Opened Chica Custom Cycles
in Huntington Beach, California

First Chica Bike on the cover of
Street Chopper magazine

W9-BJB-626

CHICA

Won Best of Show at Irvine Bike Show

First Bike Feature in *Biker* magazine

1995   **1998** **1999** **2000**

Opened Covington Cycle City

Won First Place
Daytona Master's
Bike Show

First Bike Feature
in *Easyriders* magazine

JERRY
COVINGTON

1993   **1995**

Opened new Ness Facility
in Dublin, CA

CORY
NESS

2003

Opened new
Cycle Fabrications
facility

DAVE
PEREWITZ

2005

MONDO
PORRAS

Built first custom bike
(ground-up custom fabrication)

Won best in show at the
L.A. Calendar Show

First bike on the cover of *Hot Bike*
magazine

Opened Rooke Customs

JESSE
ROOKE

2002   **2003**

Built first custom bike (Sportster)

First bike feature in *Hot Bike* magazine

Won AMA
250 GP Championship

First bike on the cover
of *Hot Rod Bike* magazine

ROLAND
SANDS

1996 **1998**   **2002**

TOP C

MASTER CHOPPER BUILDERS

HOPS

DAVE NICHOLS & MICHAEL LICHTER

MOTORBOOKS

First published in 2005 by Motorbooks, an imprint of MBI Publishing Company, Galtier Plaza, Suite 200, 380 Jackson Street, St. Paul, MN 55101-3885 USA

© Dave Nichols and Michael Lichter, 2005

All rights reserved. With the exception of quoting brief passages for the purposes of review, no part of this publication may be reproduced without prior written permission from the Publisher.

The information in this book is true and complete to the best of our knowledge. All recommendations are made without any guarantee on the part of the author or Publisher, who also disclaim any liability incurred in connection with the use of this data or specific details.

This publication has been prepared solely by MBI Publishing Company and is not approved or licensed by any other entity. We recognize that some words, model names, and designations mentioned herein are the property of the trademark holder. We use them for identification purposes only. This is not an official publication.

Motorbooks titles are also available at discounts in bulk quantity for industrial or sales-promotional use. For details write to Special Sales Manager at MBI Publishing Company, Galtier Plaza, Suite 200, 380 Jackson Street, St. Paul, MN 55101-3885 USA.

ON THE COVER: This Dave Perewitz chopper wears the master builder's trademark flame paint.

ISBN-13: 978-0-7603-2297-0
ISBN-10: 0-7603-2297-X

Editor: Darwin Holmstrom
Designer: Rochelle Schultz

Printed in China

WE WOULD LIKE TO DEDICATE this book to all the custom motorcycle builders in the world and to those who dream to create their own two-wheeled masterpieces. Special thanks to the men who inspired us for this work: Chica, Jerry Covington, Arlen and Cory Ness, Dave Perewitz, Mondo Porras, Jesse Rooke, and Roland Sands. We also thank all those who helped us track down photos of these builders including Kathleen Covington, the Ness family, Jody Perewitz, the Rooke brothers, and Ted Sands.

Much respect goes out to the staff of *Easyriders* and *V-Twin* magazines, and sincere thanks to our editor at Motorbooks, Darwin Holmstrom. A tip of the hat goes to executive producers of The Discovery Channel's *Biker Build-Off* TV series Thom Beers and Hugh King for making many of our friends into media stars. And lastly, to the intrepid Steve Temple for keeping Mr. Lichter on the straight and narrow, and much love to our dear wives Diane and Catherine for inspiring us to do what we dream.

...and to a dog named Blue, eternal thanks for all the darshan.

—Dave Nichols and Michael Lichter

CONTENTS

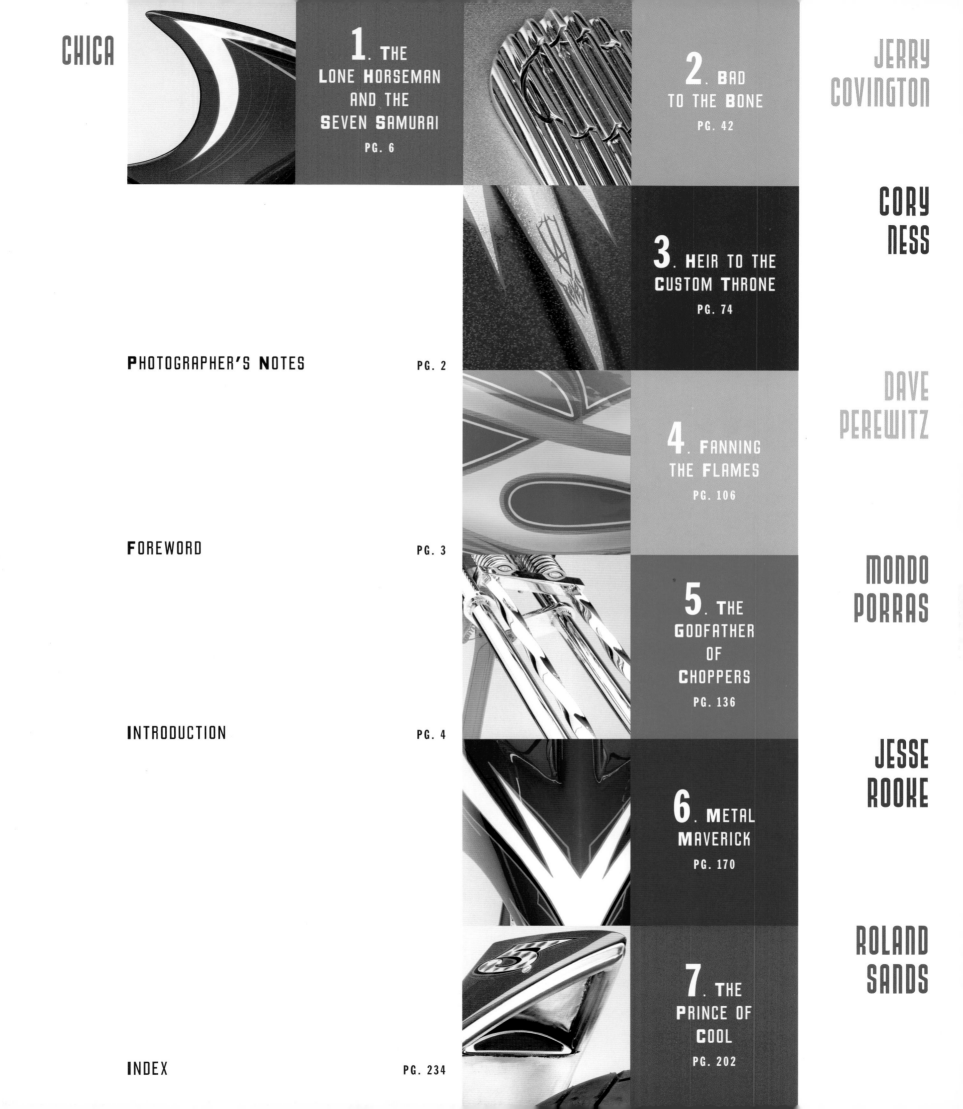

PHOTOGRAPHER'S NOTES

CAMERAS, BACKGROUNDS, AND THE STYLE OF PHOTOGRAPHY HAVE CHANGED SINCE I STARTED RIDING AND PHOTOGRAPHING CHOPPERS IN THE 1970S. The changes in photography have been enormous. Through most of the 1970s, I shot with one 35mm camera mounted with a 35mm lens and loaded with black-and-white film. By the early 1980s, I was on assignment for *Easyriders* and shooting color slide film in addition to black and white. I used multiple camera bodies and a barrage of lenses. By 1982, bike features entered my repertoire. I began shooting in my own studio (the same studio I still shoot in) with medium format 6x6cm Hasselblad cameras using quartz lights at first and then studio strobes. In the late 1980s, I started using slightly larger Mamiya cameras with their 6x7cm image, and solid painted backgrounds gave way to large hand-painted canvases. By 1998, the Mamiya gave way to big Fuji 6x8cm cameras, and the painted muslins were put away as I returned to painting the studio and shooting bike features on plain backgrounds.

A question that often comes up is why I shoot most of my bike features in the studio on plain backgrounds. For me, the *bike* is the art. I am just a facilitator, translating the three-dimensional piece to two dimensions and bringing it to the public eye. By controlling the light and the background, the focus stays on the bike. I have always felt chrome looks better with smooth neutral reflections that help shape the metal rather than strong colored reflections, green grass, or asphalt. As for camera angles, I spend way too much time on my knees and lying on my stomach, but looking up at a bike makes it seem even more monumental. It puts a little twist on what is normally seen from eye level and hopefully creates more interest for the viewer. It is about power and grace, muscle and style.

I brought the most significant photographic change upon myself in 2000 when I began shooting digital. A loyal Kodak film user for over thirty years, my film purchases began to decline slowly and steadily until by 2003 they hit zero. In the studio, I use a Leaf Scitex digital camera system with a large liquid-cooled chip in the back and Nikon lenses up front. I could put the digital back on any of my medium-format camera bodies or larger 4x5 cameras but choose to run it with an integrated live video system. There isn't even a viewfinder to look through on this beast but it sure does scream! Everything is done on the computer, composing, adjusting, capturing, processing, and archiving. In the field, I shoot with two Nikon D1Xs. To process the large quantity of raw images I generate, I have a number of Apple Macintosh computers. What may be more interesting than this technical laundry list is just imagining packing a Harley for a road trip with two of these sophisticated Nikon digital cameras, two titanium Macintosh laptop computers, back-up hard drives, more than five spare lenses, strobes, camera supports, bags, and plenty of miscellaneous gear. Clothing and toiletries get stuffed wherever they fit. It really is quite an achievement!

I have come a long way since just shooting images for myself. In addition to shooting bikes, motorcycle events for *Easyriders*, and brochures and catalogues for manufacturers, I have returned to exhibiting work from my archive in galleries and museums. I couldn't do it all without help. I took on my first full-time assistant in the mid-1980s and have had at least one assistant on my staff ever since. Steve Temple has been with me since 1999 and does an incredible job keeping all this digital equipment running—and me shooting. I have affectionately dubbed him the "Wizard." He deserves a lot of credit.

If you are interested in reading more about my work and seeing more imagery, you can visit my website at www.lichterphoto.com.

—*Michael Lichter*

FOREWORD

I USED TO FLIP THROUGH MOTORCYCLE MAGAZINES LIKE *EASYRIDERS*, STUDYING THE BIKES, IN AWE AT THE WORKMANSHIP I SAW IN THE PHOTOGRAPHS. I was just a service mechanic with no fabricating experience or skill. The Internet didn't exist, and The Discovery Channel was focused on subjects like King Tut's riches and the search for the *Titanic*. I had no ambition to become a custom motorcycle builder and never imagined getting a bike on the cover of a magazine, much less being on TV. Working on Harleys was my way of earning a living while I attended college. I didn't know then that custom motorcycles and the people who love them would change my life.

The dominant styles of custom bikes at the time were low-slung, stretched Softails with extensive sheetmetal bodywork or long rubber-mounted bikes using Arlen Ness frames. People laughed at my 1950 Panhead chopper. I never cared though, because I knew it was cool. I just didn't know how cool it would become.

I'd experimented a little with fabrication, making a few small custom pieces for my Pan. It was time, I thought, to take a shot at building a full-blown, ground-up custom. After begging my dad to lend me the money, I bought a 1972 FLH that would be the donor for my custom chopper.

The people at the Charlotte *Easyriders* bike show sent me home with my head down the year before. The custom entry I'd built for a friend didn't trophy. What I considered to be my best effort hadn't impressed anyone there—that motivated me. I also sold my last and only valuable possession. Giving up my Panhead was difficult to do, but it motivated me further. I was determined to see my '72 Shovel chop in *Easyriders*' pages. Dave Nichols and Michael Lichter saw it at the show in Charlotte and immediately wanted to photograph it. My Shovel appeared in *Biker* magazine later that year. That actually meant more to me than seeing it in *Easyriders* would have, since *Biker* is the more hardcore of the two publications. My goal had been met, and my life had changed.

Every builder who has achieved even a moderate level of success has a story as interesting and unique as mine. And each builder's creations are, in some way, reflections of their own story. Chica is from Japan, where aftermarket resources aren't as abundant as in the States. His bikes have always featured more handmade parts than most customs. A guy like Jerry Covington, who has been building bikes since before I was born, builds traditionally styled bikes with a coveted refinement. Class, humility, and pure talent have kept him at the top for years. Cory Ness' notoriety for being a successful businessman sometimes overshadows the fact that he is first and foremost a motorcycle customizer with a remarkable pedigree. One look at the bikes in these pages will show you that he's one of the best. Look at the bikes Dave Perewitz built last year and compare them to the bikes he built 25 years ago. The evolution in his work maps changes in the custom motorcycle scene that most people don't even know about. Speaking of history and legends,

we still have guys around like Mondo Porras of Denver's Choppers. I could sit for hours and listen to Mondo telling stories of the old days of choppers; the photos hanging on the walls of his shop substantiate every word. Jesse Rooke is half Mondo's age, but he has stepped into the top level of the custom bike world quicker than anyone I have ever seen. In a stale world of cheap copies, his style is fresh and welcome. The racing influence has always led the world of customizers, and Roland Sands carries that element across the finish line. His high-horsepower, bare-bones approach to performance-oriented customs blows the bondo off the competition. These are seven guys who did a whole lot more than just get lucky.

Thanks to guys like Dave Nichols and Michael Lichter for noticing and capturing on film the works of guys like myself and the Lucky Seven. The world knows who we are because of their efforts. A book like this preserves and perpetuates our craft, and leaves blank pages for the next Lucky Seven.

—Billy Lane

THE LUCKY SEVEN

SUNLIGHT STROBES THROUGH A PICKET FENCE AS YOU BLAST BY, THE MAGICAL CACOPHONY OF YOUR CHOPPER'S MOTOR THUNDERING ACROSS THE LANDSCAPE. You are one with your machine, your senses heightened as incredible sights, sounds, and scents combine in a rich mélange. Your heart beats in rhythm with the engine, and in this special place, time does not exist. Your perceptions are razor sharp, your mood is mellow, and you can't wipe the smile off of your bug-splattered face.

This is the ride and you are in the zone, a true centaur blending human and motorcycle, and *this* is what life is all about. Everyday worries are left behind as you sweep through a curve. Thoughts of mortgage payments, bills for the kid's braces, and the war on terror are miles away. Now you understand why riding a custom bike is synonymous with freedom. For this supreme moment, you are living your dream.

Welcome to *Top Chops*, wherein we take a look at today's master bike builders, men who live their dreams every day of the week. Most people who have taken on the occupation of custom motorcycle builder truly love their job. You never hear complaints about having to stay an extra hour to route the wires through a frame or spend a weekend at a custom bike show. No, motorcycles are the lifeblood of bike builders, and the seven builders who grace these pages would tell you that motorcycles are their passion in life—bikes keep their blood pumping.

The seven gentlemen chosen by Michael Lichter and myself for this book are not only exceptional bike builders; they epitomize men who truly live their dreams. They get up in the morning, excited to get to work each day, spend every waking hour thinking about building wild custom choppers, and at night they dream of their next innovation or twisted design. For these reasons and more, we call these men the Lucky Seven. Each of them has become a household name, thanks to the amazing medium of television, and they have had their fabled 15 minutes of fame, thanks to the Discovery Channel's popular *Biker Build-Off* television series. Let's meet them.

YASUYOSHI CHIKAZAWA, formerly of Japan and currently of Huntington Beach, California, is known worldwide simply as Chica. If a custom bike is built by Chica Custom Cycles, you may be guaranteed that it is a one-of-a-kind wonder of metal and magic, hand-hewn by the moto-master himself.

JERRY COVINGTON hails from Woodward, Oklahoma, and is known for his sleek designed scoots that run the gamut from old school bobbers and choppers, to hot rod pro-street pavement pounders. Like many of our Lucky Seven, Jerry and his crew at Covington's Cycle City never build the same bike twice.

CORY NESS is the heir apparent of the Arlen Ness dynasty. He has been around custom bikes since the day of his birth and has designed many of the custom parts and accessories that make up the Ness catalog. Besides running the family business, Cory builds exotic custom bikes that are known for their quality and excellent fit and finish.

DAVE PEREWITZ of Brockton, Massachusetts, is one of the true kings of customizing, standing alongside such master builders as Arlen Ness and Donnie Smith. He conjures up everything from lavish flame jobs to long and lean asphalt eaters, complete and ready for the road from his shop, Cycle Fabrications.

No book about the Lucky Seven custom bike builders would be complete without including the godfather of choppers, **MONDO PORRAS.** Mondo has been creating hand-built custom choppers the old school way since 1967 at Denver's Choppers (currently in Henderson, Nevada). Mondo carries on after the fatal speedboat crash of Denver Mullins in 1997. Without Mondo, those sexy long bikes known as choppers would have never evolved.

Metal maverick **JESSE ROOKE** appeared out of the Arizona desert a few years ago, riding a mind-blowing custom creation that turned the heads of even the world's most jaded moto journalists at the Del Mar Motorcycle Races and Bike Show. Jesse is known for his wild style of lithe scooters that marry classic Stingray bicycle style to the latest technology to create something entirely new in the custom universe.

ROLAND SANDS is one of the young guns of motorcycle design. The son of Perry Sands, owner of Performance Machine in La Palma, California, Roland grew up as the proverbial kid in the custom candy store. His love for racing motorcycles led him to design many of the parts and products for Performance Machine as well as to complete mind-melting custom creations.

Together, our Lucky Seven bend steel in their bare hands, leap tall Neilsen ratings with a single bound, and present us with incredible custom bikes . . . the American way. Yes, these are the wizards who give birth to today's Top Chops.

THE LONE HORSEMAN
AND THE SEVEN SAMURAI

FIREBALL

OWNER: Frank Cotroneo

YEAR OF BUILD: 2004

ENGINE: S&S Shovel

FRAME: Chica

SPECIAL FEATURES: Glass oil tank; nitrous; split rocker covers with "devil's ears."

CHICA'S *FIREBALL*

Chica named this bike after its one-of-a-kind blown glass oil tank. Yes, you can actually see the oil bubbling inside the tank! This was Chica's second *Biker Build-Off* scooter and it lost to Mike Pugliese of New York's one-off wonder. From the unique hand-hewn gas tank and rear fender to the Chica single downtube frame, this bike is an ode to the kind of attention to detail that is pure Chica all the way.

The motor for this red demon is an S&S Cycle 93-cubic inch Shovelhead featuring a nitrous tank for a little extra oomph! You can bet this pavement pounder runs as good as it looks! Most everything else on the bike, save for the Performance Machine brakes and Paughco springer front end, was made by Chica, including the one-off exhaust pipes.

FIREBALL

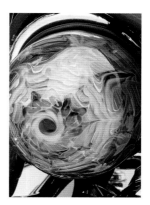

Ready to get to work in Kyoto. Chica paid his dues at several bike shops before starting his own.
Chikazawa family archive

CHICA

THERE HAVE BEEN MANY UNIQUE OPPORTUNITIES FOR EAST TO MEET WEST OVER THE PAST 50 YEARS AND VISA VERSA. Certainly one of the most enduring ways for these very different cultures to clash or combine has been through the wonder of cinema. Imagine a young Japanese child, perhaps eight years old, sitting in a tiny theater somewhere in Osaka, the silver screen awash in very Western images. Yul Brynner and James Coburn exchange squinty stares and minimal dialog as the heroes of *The Magnificent Seven* are collected to do their mercenary best.

We all know the classic tale: A town besieged by outlaws hires seven gunmen. The best way to fight an outlaw is with your own outlaws. The film's

popularity in Japan was fitting; the plot of this famous American western was borrowed from a famous Japanese film, *The Seven Samurai*. But as young Yasuyoshi Chikazawa watched the laconic gunmen, his thoughts were only of the modern west. Chica, as his friends call him, often wondered about America, that fabled land of opportunity where a man could live life his own way and make his own kind of art. In Chica's case, art and motorcycles were intimately linked.

Chica's passion for Harley-Davidsons began in the 1980s, when a close friend allowed him to ride his FXR. It has often been said that bikers get bitten by the Harley bug, and this was certainly true of Chica. He became obsessed with all things on two wheels. He began reading every issue of *Easyriders* magazine that he could lay hands on. The magazine was, and is, a biker's bible of sorts. Every page showcases gorgeous custom choppers, beautiful women, and the two-wheeled lifestyle. In short, Chica became a biker in his late teens. The greaser style of 1950s Americana appealed to the young rider. He became

By the early 1980s, the motorcycle bug had bit Chica. He soon discovered that there's nothing like getting some wind.
Chikazawa family archive

the laconic gunman of the American westerns, but with a faithful motorcycle instead of a horse beneath him.

When asked what his parents thought about his riding motorcycles, Chica puts on a good imitation of his mom and dad shouting, "No way, you'll kill yourself!" Of his two brothers, Chica's younger brother rides dirt bikes, and Chica himself admits to loving all kinds of motorcycles—"Dirt bikes, sportbikes, choppers, everything!"

Like many teenagers, Chica developed a need for speed that evolved into his personal passion for motorcycles. "I loved how fast they went and how alive I felt when I was riding," Chica says.

This rebel with a cause began working at local Honda shops near Osaka and learning more about the wrenching side of the biker's life. Chica's very first custom Harley was entirely built by hand. It had all the classic elements of a chopper. Beginning with a rigid frame, Chica scrounged for parts and came up with a Sportster gas tank and a Narrow Glide front end. He handmade the fenders and found a used Shovelhead motor from an old FXE model. The builder has always had a warm spot in his heart for older Harley motors. The old Panheads and Shovelheads just seem to have a heart beating inside their metal skin. They have character, and they demand respect. If you don't treat them properly, they will happily leave you by the side of the road.

Young Chica circa 1982,
a proud rider with leathers
to match his red-and-white
in-line four.
Chikazawa family archive

A ride on a friend's Harley inspired Chica to build his own.
Here we see him tooling down the highway on a
Harley-Davidson FLST, looking cool. *Chikazawa family archive*

In 1990, Chica went to work for a Harley-Davidson dealership in Kyoto.
As he spent his time learning the ins and outs of wrenching on old Harleys, he
began to form a plan in his mind. You see, finding Harley parts in Japan
was—and is—a real hassle. Parts are rare and very expensive. Then once you
have a bike together, getting it registered and insured is a major, and even more
expensive, hassle. Images of the American West mixed with American pop
culture in Chica's mind: Clint Eastwood lighting a cigarro with a wooden match;
James Dean pulling up the collar on his leather jacket; Marlon Brando scrapping
with Lee Marvin over a dame in a tight sweater; Elvis belting out "Jailhouse
Rock." The seeds that were planted in that movie theater in Osaka began
to germinate, and Chica was soon on his way to sunny California—land of sun,
bikinis, hot rods, and choppers!

It was 1997 and the average biker had no idea that a man from Japan was
about to rock the custom world. Chica took a job at a Southern California Harley
dealership and began plying his trade. Over time, he put aside parts for his own
kind of custom bike. He had learned to be thrifty from his years of scrounging
for rare parts in Japan, and though parts were far more plentiful in California,
Chica still did things his way. His bike would be sparse; just a frame, a motor,
and wheels. His chopper would have heart and would act as a slap in the face to
builders who throw together $70,000 custom choppers. Rather than use an

OWNER: Kent Stevens

YEAR OF BUILD: 2003

ENGINE: 1957 Harley-Davidson Panhead

FRAME: Chica

SPECIAL FEATURES: Uses 18-inch wheels front and rear.

BLACK BOBBER

$8,000–$10,000 aftermarket motor, Chica would use the old Harley motors that he was fond of, Panheads and Shovelheads that he could afford to buy. By 1998, Chica Custom Cycles was humbly born in Huntington Beach.

The business began as a restoration and repair shop for older Harleys. Over time it evolved into Chica's custom shop for his own unique creations. Today, the business is also known as a fabrication house for Chica's line of aftermarket products and accessories.

Chica began showing his custom bikes at the *Easyriders* Bike Show in Pomona. I remember the first bike that Chica ever wheeled into the enormous Fairplex. There, beside lavish and overdone glitz customs, sat a simple and

BLACK BOBBER

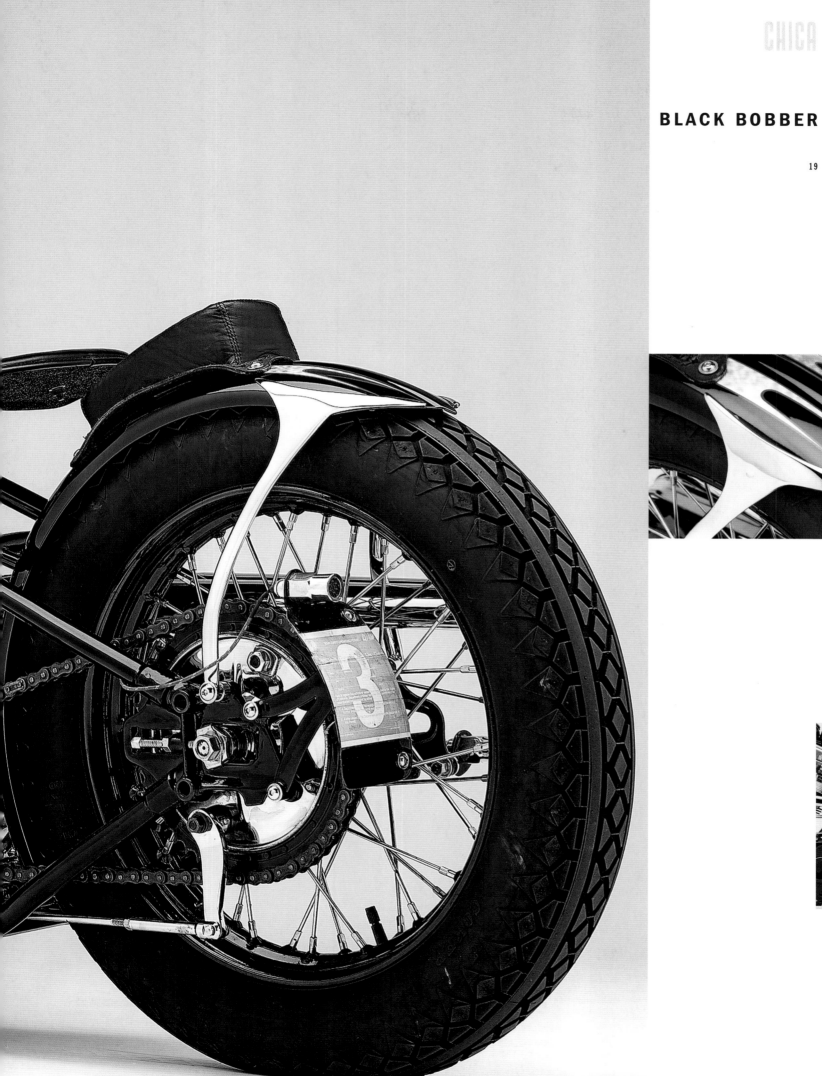

The "Chica look" burst on the American custom-bike scene in the late 1990s. As with this early Shovelhead, all of Chica's bikes were showstoppers. *Chikazawa family archive*

An early Chica custom chopper greets the sunlight for the first time.

elegant black chopper. Every part was hewn by hand, and there was blood and sweat in every nut and bolt on the bike. That 1979 Shovelhead chopper won Third Place in the Judged Specialty Class in 1999 and made it to the cover of *Easyriders* (the very wish book that Chica used to dream over back in Osaka) in August of 2000. The feature was called "Badness in Black."

"While gone are the days of the kickass chopper built from a basketcase traded for a few cases of beer, it is refreshing to know that there are bike builders out there who still carry on the tradition in a day where billet and chrome have hoped to replace form and function," said writer Erik Falconer. He went on to point out all the beautiful handmade details, including the one-off handlebars by Chica, Denver's Choppers Springer front end, and rigid frame. That was the beginning of a very long line of bike features in custom bike magazines all over the world.

Since that first chopper graced the pages of *Easyriders*, Chica has handcrafted about 50 custom motorcycles, building only 8 to 10 per year. Each is a true work of art that speaks volumes about the man himself. Each is a functional, rolling mechanical masterpiece.

When Chica came to America, he only spoke a little English. He let his bikes speak for him, and speak they did. They told tales of a once and future America,

The family Chikazawa—(from left to right) Chica's wife Hitomi, one-year-old Ace, three-year-old Johnny, and six-year old-Claudia—enjoying a Southern California sunset on the beach.

a land of opportunity and freedom, a place of vast expanses where one man on two wheels could still carve a proud, unique, and successful niche with his own two hands.

Even today, Chica likes to do things his way. He chain smokes as he sits cross-legged on the floor in front of the bike he is working on. He doesn't even own a bike lift to get the scoot up in the air. He is the only builder in this country that I know of who spreads his tools out in front of him on a cloth and works on the bike right on the floor, just the way they used to do it in Japan. A true craftsman, he begins every custom bike with simple, elegant drawings. The finished bikes look remarkably like their initial musings from the master. Chica will look at his drawing of an unusual gas tank or fender and then go to work with flat sheet metal, cutting and carving, bending and smoothing the raw materials into his works of art.

Each new custom bike told us more about Chica. His wild *Hot Lava* Knuckle-head chopper appeared on the cover of the May 2001 issue of *Easyriders*. The bike took an impressive Third Place Best of Show in Pomona, and in the Bike Show coverage in the same issue, there is a very rare photo of Chica . . . smiling. You see, Chica is often deep in thought and appears to be scowling. I remember handing out the trophies at the bike show and looking out at the faces in the

BLACK GOOSENECK

OWNER: Tim Mullins

YEAR OF BUILD: 2005

ENGINE: S&S bottom end with Flathead Power Knuckle-style top end

FRAME: Chica

SPECIAL FEATURES: Hurst shifter from Mopar muscle car; Chica-trademark stylized Z-bar handlebar and ornate headlight bracket.

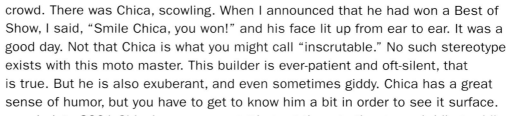

crowd. There was Chica, scowling. When I announced that he had won a Best of Show, I said, "Smile Chica, you won!" and his face lit up from ear to ear. It was a good day. Not that Chica is what you might call "inscrutable." No such stereotype exists with this moto master. This builder is ever-patient and oft-silent, that is true. But he is also exuberant, and even sometimes giddy. Chica has a great sense of humor, but you have to get to know him a bit in order to see it surface.

In late 2001 Chica's name was getting out there to the general riding public, and Ed Martin of Chrome Specialties had Chica create a cool bobber from many parts in the Chrome Specialties catalog. The bike appeared in the July 2001 issue of *Easyriders* and launched Chica's line of aftermarket parts. Chica was building his own frames, handlebars, gas and oil tanks, fenders, front ends, and wheels with more parts on the way. He was also defining the "Chica look" of his bobberesque little pavement pounders.

At the next Pomona Bike Show in 2002, Chica took a Second Place Best of Show for his tribute to Von Dutch. This flat black bombshell thumbed its nose at all the Easter egg–colored customs and established Chica as the true bad boy of bobbers.

The August 2002 issue of *Easyriders* offered up a first for the builder from Osaka. His Howler drag bike showcased an 80-ci Harley Evolution motor in its nimble Santee frame. When you think of a Chica bike, your mind might come

BLACK GOOSENECK

Riding the roads of
California. Nothing captures
the old-school attitude
better than a Chica bike.
Chikazawa family archive

Moving into the first shop in
Huntington Beach, California,
soon to be filled with
chopper-building activity.
Chikazawa family archive

Welcome to America, land
of endless Harley parts. A
pile of engine cases to
some is true gold for Chica.
Chikazawa family archive

closer to the scoots seen in the July 2003 issue of *Easyriders*. Here Chica
scores another cover and an unprecedented *two* bikes in the same issue. His
long and low digger and lean chopper-style bikes, both dressed in black with
subtle old school graphics, used standard 80-inch Harley Evo motors. But these
customs were a departure from using classic H-D motors and were rare in
Chica's stable.

By this time Chica was a well-known builder in Southern California. His parts
and products, and yes, even T-shirts, were hot items. But there was still more on
the horizon for Chikazawa-san.

Here we must pause for a moment to take note of a strange phenomenon
that took place in the early twenty-first century. You see, there was once
a television series called *On the Inside*, which took in-depth looks at odd
occupations. They had featured a rodeo clown and an underwater welder and
were looking for a custom bike builder for their next episode. Television producer
Hugh King called me up (Hugh had worked as a video editor for *Easyriders*
several years before) and asked me to help him find just the right builder for
the program. This builder had to be young, out of control, and work in Southern
California. I took Hugh to see Jesse James at West Coast Choppers in Long
Beach. I pointed out the shark tank, the pitbulls, the spider web fencing, and
Jesse. Hugh knew instantly that Jesse would be "good TV" and the *On The Inside*

Chica has always been a fan of classic American choppers. He's seen here on a Denver's-style Frisco chop with 16-inch over springer.
Chikazawa family archive

HARD ROCK CRUISER

OWNER: Chica

YEAR OF BUILD: 2004

ENGINE: S&S 93-inch Shovel

FRAME: Chica

SPECIAL FEATURES: Built for the Seminal Hard Rock Casino and Hotel Tour; hand-crafted single-downtube frame with molded-in fuel tank pays homage to 1970s-style long bike.

show became *Motorcycle Mania*, which aired on the Discovery Channel. The episode brought in the highest ratings ever for a cable network show. Naturally, *Motorcycle Mania Part Two* and *Three* followed, as did the *Monster Garage* TV series and the rest, as they say, is history.

But wait, there's more. Once the suits in Maryland (where the Discovery Channel is based) realized that Americans had an instant love affair with two wheels, Hugh King went on to produce the popular *Biker Build-Off* series for The Discovery Channel. It should be noted that Hugh works for Thom Beers of Original Productions and that all the series mentioned so far are under the

Chica Custom Cycles opened in Huntington Beach, California, in 1998. Chikazawa-san hasn't looked back since. *Chikazawa family archive*

Original Productions banner. Hugh is now the coexecutive producer with Beers on the *Biker Build-Off* series.

As fate, or luck, would have it, when Hugh needed expert master bike builders to design and build a custom motorcycle against the clock (TV just *loves* when things happen against the clock), he would call me and ask, "Who's hot? Who's next?" So, dear readers, for good or ill, you have me to thank or blame for bringing such diverse and wondrous builders as Billy Lane, Paul Yaffe, Dave Perewitz, Mitch Bergeron, Jerry Covington, Kendall Johnson, and others to the small screen. Sorry guys, I know the TV sword is double edged at times and fame has its price.

One of these wondrous builders was, yes, you are way ahead of me, Chica. The fascinating thing about Chica is that, having survived a brush of fame (enduring more than his fair 15 minutes promised by Andy Warhol) he has not changed one bit. He is the same centered, nonplussed bike builder whom I met many moons ago.

Chica is somewhat guarded about his family life. We know he is married with four children. When asked if his wife likes motorcycles he says, "She is not

too crazy about motorcycles, because they are too loud." When asked if his children ride, he smiles and says, "Not yet."

A very popular bike, and one that appeared in the May 2005 issue of *Easyriders*, is his Unicorn bike. This was the sled that was first unveiled on the *Biker Build-Off* series. Every piece of this motorcycle was made by hand, the old-fashioned, tried-and-true way. Picture Chica sitting on his mat before this brilliant blue steed, coaxing it to life, piece by piece.

What about bike building heroes? Has Chica been influenced by any of today's custom builders? He sums this up with two words, "Arlen Ness." Does Chica have advice to give to any other builders out there? "I don't have any

BLACK LONGBIKE

OWNER: Billy Tropp

YEAR OF BUILD: 2003

ENGINE: Patrick Racing 124-inch Evo-type

FRAME: Chica

SPECIAL FEATURES: One of the few bikes in which Chica used an Evolution-type engine.

OWNER: Richard Schwartz

YEAR OF BUILD: 2004

ENGINE: S&S Shovel

FRAME: Chica

SPECIAL FEATURES: Diamond theme used in bike at request of the owner; only Chica bike to use a Paul Cox seat.

advice for the other builders, because they all have amazing skill, and their own styles and ideas."

Does luck enter into the precise world of motorized marvels that Chica has created? If so, it is the luck of being able to live each day doing what you love most to do. All of the builders in this tome have that in common. From a young lad in Osaka dreaming of America and custom machines that he is only now fashioning into amazing moving sculptures, Chica is surely one of the Lucky Seven.

The Seven Samurai, the Magnificent Seven, the Lucky Seven. Coincidence? Perhaps, but for this honest bike builder there is only one way he wishes to be remembered: "No stereotypes, no zen master, not samurai, not kamikaze, not old school, just Chica!"

And so it is. ✪

OWNER: Dr. Chris Vigil

YEAR OF BUILD: 2003

ENGINE: S&S bottom end with Flathead Power Knuckle-style top end

FRAME: Chica

SPECIAL FEATURES: Built for anesthesiologist—hence the name "Ether"; rear fender stand recalls to an earlier time.

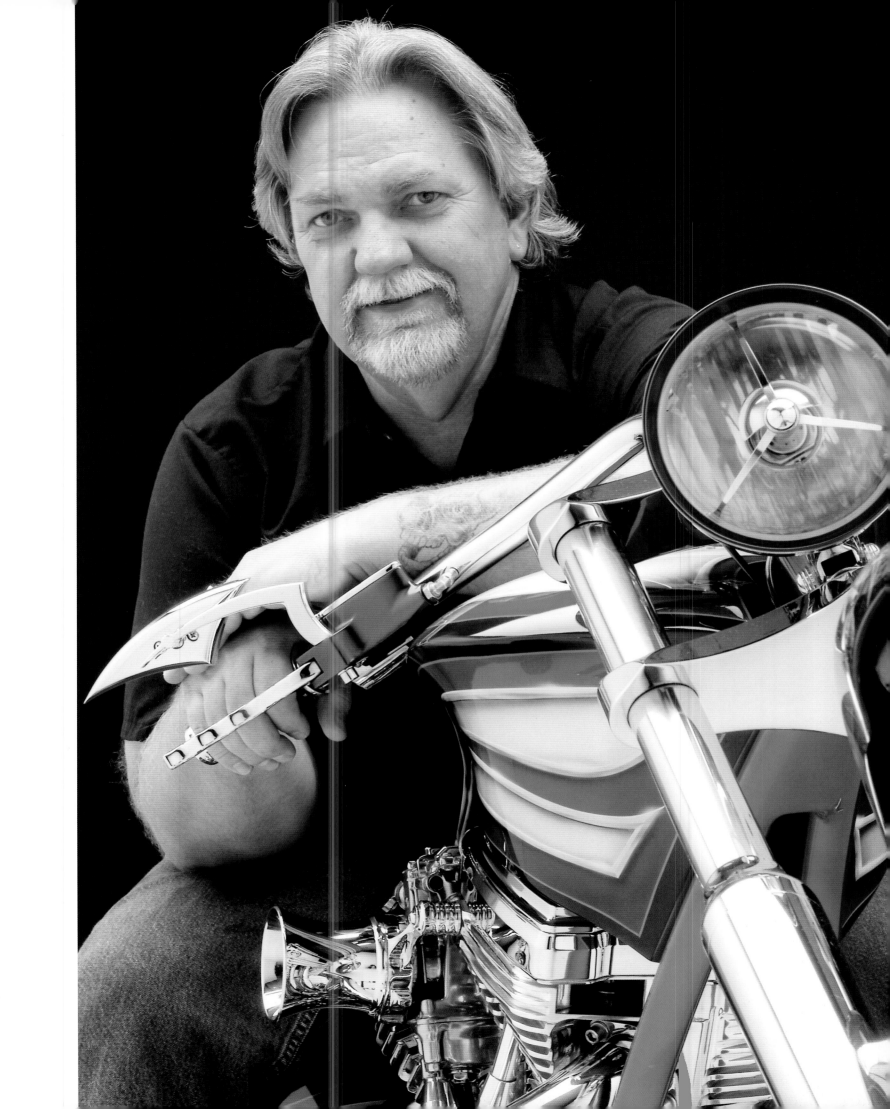

BAD TO THE BONE

OWNER: Jerry Covington

YEAR OF BUILD: 2004

ENGINE: Patrick Racing 113-inch Evo-type

FRAME: Covington Hot Rod Softail

SPECIAL FEATURES: Floating fender attached to swingarm; custom-designed three-dimensional triple tree; nitrous; hand-made multi-piece wheels; hand-made gas tank; custom air suspension.

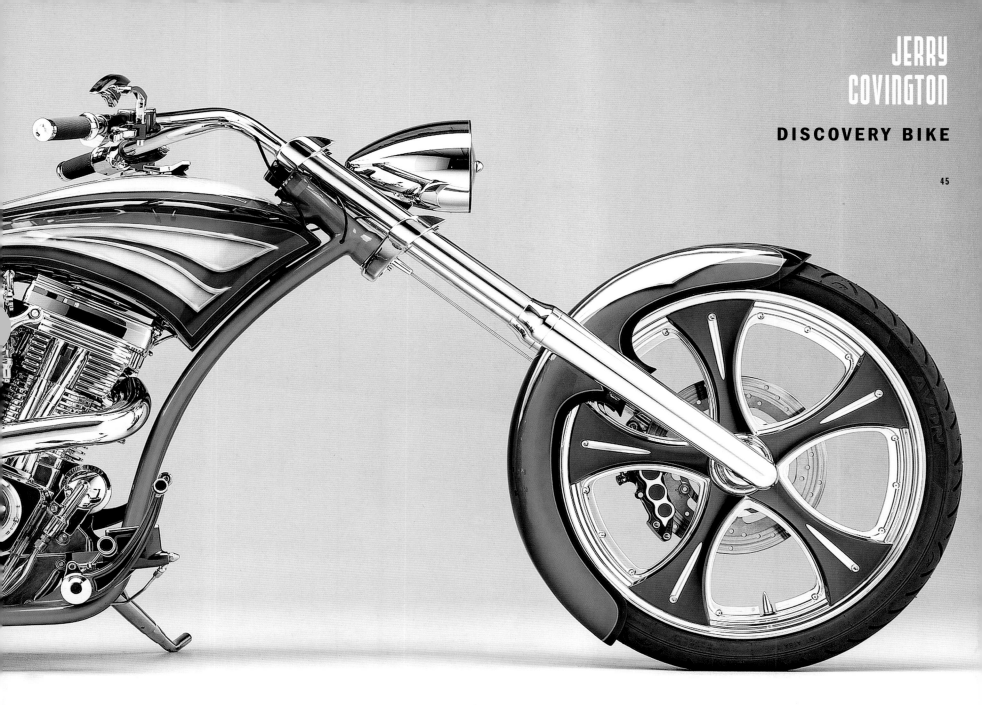

JERRY COVINGTON'S *TOXIC*

Known for his sleek, pro-street designs, Jerry Covington won his *Biker Build-Off* episode against Warren Vesley of Scooter Shooterz with this wild green machine. The hidden-shock frame, tanks, fenders, and wheels are all cool Covington designs. Because of the massive 300 rear tire, Jerry went with a Baker Right Side Drive transmission to keep the bike balanced and going down the road straight. Special thanks go to Nigel Patrick for the bulletproof Patrick Racing 113-cubic inch billet motor with Nitrous Express go juice.

All the sheetmetal fabrication was done in-house in just ten days and John Stromberg of Lucky 7 Custom Paint handled the magnificent paint job that acts as the icing on the cake for this classy creation.

The two iron horsemen ride in for the Build-Off competition. Jerry on his Toxic green pro-street bike, and Warren Vesley on his fire-breathing demon. *Covington family archive*

JERRY COVINGTON

WE BEGAN OUR CHAPTER ON CHICA BY ASKING YOU TO IMAGINE A YOUNG BOY IN A DARK MOVIE THEATER. Oddly enough, this chapter begins with a boy also, but 10-year-old Jerry Covington is in a bright and warm garage, chopping a bicycle all to pieces. The innovative lad is replacing the stock front forks with long, spindly ones that he fashioned out of some discarded lawn furniture. As with many custom builders, the spark of creation began burning with Jerry's first breath, and the blazing fire of artistic design has yet to be extinguished.

Jerry was born in Cleburne, Texas, but grew up in sunny Southern California, land of hot rods and birthplace of choppers. Jerry is the youngest in a family of four sisters and two brothers and the only one who was bitten by the California

Top Row: Dusty Brown, David Covington, Pee Wee Covington, Jerry Covington, Cameron Brown. Bottom Row: Kim Brown, Rochelle Covington, Kathleen Covington, Sarah Brown. *Covington family archive*

Jerry does a nasty burnout on his Discovery Channel Toxic Shocker. Never let it be said that Jerry Covington doesn't know how to have a good time. *Covington family archive*

Kustom Kulture bug. He was bitten mighty early, building and painting hot rod model kits, then turning his attention to customizing bicycles. "I think I saw my first custom motorcycle in 1968," Jerry grins. "That was it for me, I started riding when I was 11." You could say that right from the start, Jerry was bad to the bone.

As often happens when the bike bug bites a kid, Jerry's parents didn't necessarily see eye to eye on the subject of letting their youngest son ride. "My Mom always thought motorcycles were dangerous but my Dad rode bikes. He was in law enforcement, so he rode police bikes," Jerry recalls. "I have always had a passion for cars and motorcycles from as far back as I can remember. I started working on cars when I was about 10 or 11, and that eventually led me to bikes."

Jerry was actively building bikes by the time he was 18 and created his first chopper in 1973. "I used to hang out at Denver's Choppers back when they were in Riverside. I'd buy parts from Denver Mullins, Mondo Bondo, and Little Freddie. Bike builders were real bikers back then," Jerry laughs. "I traded an old

car for my first Harley-Davidson, then I chopped it, then I crashed it." Covington wound up in traction for three months and used the insurance money from the bike to buy another Harley.

From that time on, Jerry was always working on bikes and decided to turn his passion into a full-time career. In 1992 Jerry moved to Woodward, Oklahoma, and started Covington's Cycle City in 1993. "We started out just customizing stock Harleys," Jerry says. "Then, we got into building custom choppers from the ground up. Today we make all the components we can in-house along with doing our own custom paint and bodywork."

HOT ROD CHOPPER

OWNER: Ron Heate

YEAR OF BUILD: 2004

ENGINE: H&L 131-inch Evo-type billet

FRAME: Covington Chopper Softail

SPECIAL FEATURES: Handcrafted sheet metal; red anodizing; seat dropped to just 18-inches off the ground.

Covington's Cycle City is known for designing and manufacturing a wide array of parts and accessories for custom bikes. Currently, Jerry's company makes everything from their own frames, tanks, and fenders, to billet triple trees, primary covers, wheels, handlebars—you name it. Their state-of-the-art fabrication shop features the latest CNC machines in order to turn solid blocks of aircraft-quality billet aluminum into exciting new parts for custom bikes.

All of Jerry's bikes have a certain "Covington look" about them, and part of that look has to do with the incredible custom paint jobs by John Stromberg. John's company, Lucky 7 Custom Paint (another strange coincidence?)

At the end of the day, it's all about riding. Here we see Jerry tearing up the highway with his crew on new Covington bobbers.
Covington family archive

of Amarillo, Texas, is known for spraying the color on most of Jerry's award-winning rides. "I wouldn't be doing what I'm doing if it were not for Jerry," John told us. "He has really helped me along." The master painter has also painted bikes for Mark Warrick's Soncy Road, Jim Nasi Customs, Stinger Customs, and Billet-4-U.

"I enjoy doing classy, tasteful paint jobs and that is exactly what Jerry likes as well," John says, admitting that Covington has a lot of trust in his abilities. "Jerry usually just tells me what color he has in mind, and I go to town." And boy, does he ever. You could say this team is lucky to have found each other.

Covington knows that he is lucky in many ways. He is lucky to have a very supportive wife in Kathleen and five great kids. His four very creative sons also love bikes and work in the family business. "Kathleen says that she knew when she met me that if she didn't join in with the motorcycles and cars she'd be left out of the things the boys and I love," Jerry says. "She rides her own bike when she has one. You see, we have a hard time keeping one, whether it is mine or hers. We always end up selling our bikes to customers."

Kathleen actually was one of the first women to ride a chopper back in 1995 when the current chopper craze was coming on strong. "I built her a chopper back when women weren't riding as much as they are now," Jerry remembers. "Kathleen runs the office and is the shop mom; all the guys call her

mom. She loves the industry and the people." They say that behind all great men you will find a truly great woman. This adage is certainly true of Jerry and Kathleen Covington.

Jerry also knows that he is very lucky to have talented sons who work with him every day, designing and building the bikes they love. "It's really cool. I get to see my boys every day and they all have the same passion for bikes that I do. The oldest does drivetrain and assembly; the next one down does fabrication, assembly, and is my shop foreman. The next one down is body shop foreman and does body work and paint on the bikes. The youngest runs one of our CNC machines."

And Jerry's son David is becoming a master builder in his own right, creating one-off wonders that are winning Best of Show awards at bike shows across the

OWNER: Jerry Covington

YEAR OF BUILD: 2002

ENGINE: Total Performance 121-inch Evo-type

FRAME: Covington Rigid

SPECIAL FEATURES: Weber two-barrel side-draft carb; 24-karat gold leaf in paint; exhausts exit on both sides.

country. One of David's latest creations is a radical gold bobber that was my favorite bike at a recent *Easyriders* Bike Show in Atlanta. The scoot took Second Place Best of Show in the Invitational Class, marking the bike as one of the very best of the best in the entire country. Like his father, David is very humble about his building abilities, but mark my words, David Covington is one bike builder to watch in years to come.

I remember first meeting Jerry at our *Easyriders* Invitational Bike Show in Columbus, Ohio, about five years ago. This is the crème de la crème of bike shows, with the country's best builders showing off their finest stuff. Jerry was very proud of a long and lean red chopper that he built and it took home a Second Place Best of Show in the Judged Class against the very best bikes in the country. From then on, Covington has been a part of our shows every year, always winning top honors for his wild rides, which invariably end up on the cover of *Easyriders* magazine.

One such cover bike was Jerry's personal ride, a candy green old school

LUCIFER

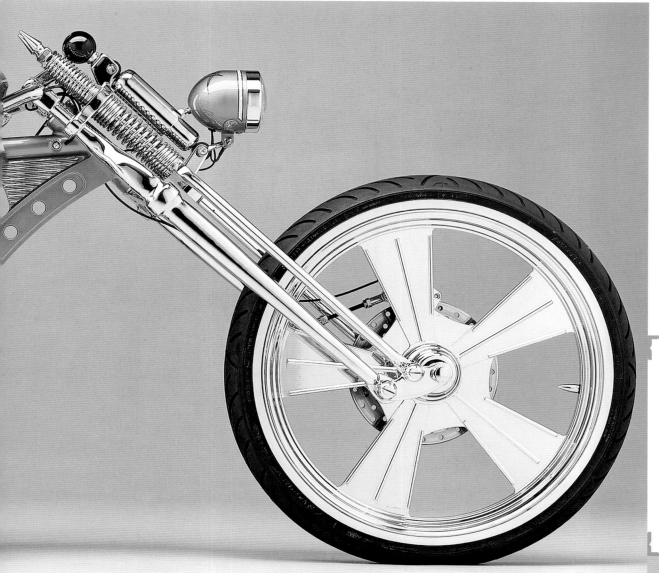

OWNER: Chris Miller

YEAR OF BUILD: 2004

ENGINE: Accurate Engineering 103-inch Panhead

FRAME: Hand crafted by David Covington

SPECIAL FEATURES: Jerry's son David's first custom; won $30,000 first prize in Texas Chop Off; spun-aluminum oil tank; dual Stromberg 97 carbs from a 1932 Ford.

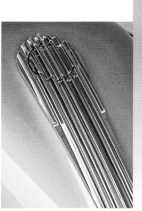

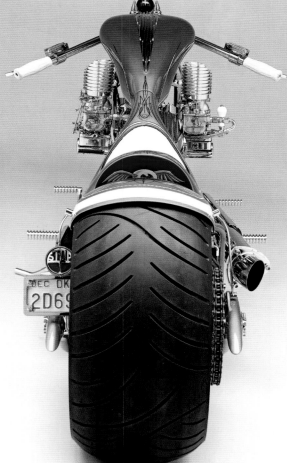

LUCIFER

Here's proof that Jerry can coax a smoking burnout even from a Harley dresser. "The owner brought the bike in to change the tires but the rear still had some tread on it. I couldn't see it going to waste," Jerry told us. *Covington family archive*

Jerry and Kathleen Covington.

chopper with an 18-inch-over-stock Denver's Choppers springer front end. The rigid framed showstopper was called *Covington's Keeper* in the May 2004 issue of *Easyriders*. "To me," Jerry told us, "this bike embodies the real spirit of a chopper, with some new twists thrown in here and there." The new twists Jerry spoke of included a 240 rear tire, a six-speed transmission, and one of TP Engineering's amazing 121-ci motors.

"Back during the early 1970s, when I was growing up in Southern California and learning about motorcycles, I built a lot of bikes that looked pretty much like that green chopper," Jerry remembers. "Some things never change."

Covington Cycle City's 16-person crew creates around 25 amazing custom bikes every year, and when asked to define his style of bike, Jerry told us, "My bikes are smooth and clean, and everything flows." As with many of today's top builders, Jerry hides all the cables, wires, and lines wherever possible. His bikes have a fluid look; every piece is thought out, everything matches the flow of the overall design.

When asked if he has been influenced by other bike builders, Jerry says, "I feel that I have always had my own designs in my head. I like many of the other builders on the scene, guys like Eddie Trotta, but I definitely listen to the beat of my own drummer." That drummer has served Jerry well. The beat of that drum is very similar to the lopping thump of a Harley-Davidson motor.

Covington bikes are all about attention to detail. Here Jerry works through the wee hours doing the electrical on this scoot. *Covington family archive*

Jerry's bikes are known for their swoopy curves and clean fitment. But Covington builds everything from old school bobbers and choppers (seen left of Jerry) to high tech wonders. *Covington family archive*

Just as Covington customs have their own distinct look, it is also hard to pin Jerry down to any specific type of bike. His stretched out pro-street diggers have become very popular, but so are his traditional choppers. Recently, Jerry and his sons have been experimenting with the old fashioned bobber-style bike. These short and very light scoots are reminiscent of the custom bikes of the 1950s and 1960s. Riders would take everything they could off their stock Harleys in order to make them lighter and faster. Bobbers were the first street fighter–style bikes; little more than an engine, a frame, a gas tank, and wheels. The only thing that all these various styles of custom bikes have in common is that they are unmistakably cool, and if it's cool, Covington is building it.

After many years of building custom bikes, Jerry is yet another of the current so-called "overnight successes" in the custom bike world. He went up against Warren Vesley in a *Biker Build-Off* episode for the Discovery Channel that first aired on January 11, 2005. Naturally, the phone began ringing off the hook, and Jerry is now a well-known face at bike shows and motorcycle rallies all across the country. As has been the case with many of the builders in this book, I had the privilege of passing Jerry's name to Hugh King, executive producer of the *Build-Off* series. Hugh was familiar with Jerry's work and thought he would be a natural.

"I just really liked the angle that Jerry is doing all this cool work from way out in Oklahoma," Hugh says. "He is proof that you don't have to live in

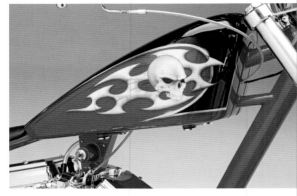

OWNER: Jim Edinger

YEAR OF BUILD: 2002

ENGINE: Patrick Racing 120-inch Evo-type

FRAME: Covington Hot Rod Softail

SPECIAL FEATURES: Eight-inch stretch on downtube;
16-inch over fork.

CLEAN SWEEP

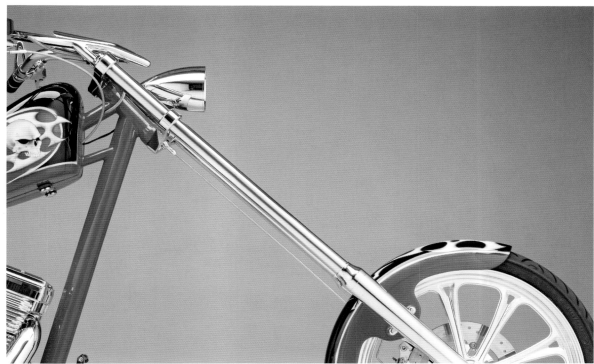

Hollywood or New York in order to turn out really innovative bikes."

One of the things I really look forward to is going to Daytona BikeWeek down in Florida each March to check out Jerry's latest customs. He and Kathleen make the trek from Oklahoma to Florida every year and are always set up in the same spot behind the Daytona Harley-Davidson dealership on Beach Street. Jerry will point to some outrageous new bike, grin, and say, "What do you think of that?" That's his way of letting you know he's a tad proud of a certain build. I always smile back and ask him if any other bike magazine has shot it yet.

Jerry's easy style and positive attitude led me to ask him to build an auction bike for the prestigious 2005 V-Twin Biker's Ball in Daytona. The wild sled he

continued on page 70

OWNER: Chris Miller

YEAR OF BUILD: 2004

ENGINE: Kendall Johnson 145-inch Evo-type

FRAME: Covington Hot Rod Softail

SPECIAL FEATURES: Michael Justus hand-tooled leather seat; pipes in tank direct cooling air to engine; extensive handcrafted metal work.

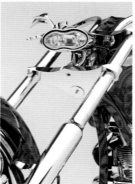

The Covington crew shares in the glory of the *Biker Build-Off* win. Son David holds the goods. *Covington family archive*

concocted brought in major money for the Boys & Girls Club. You see, besides doing very well, Jerry is the kind of guy who also likes to give back.

Naturally, when a top bike builder is in the spotlight and in the public eye as Jerry is, other builders, many of them newcomers to the custom scene, want to know how they can join the ranks of the Lucky Seven. "I always tell new builders not to expect to become a master bike builder over night," Jerry confides. "Don't mix other builders' styles together. Be original and make your own style." Then, after 30 years or so, you too might be an overnight success.

Jerry will no doubt be remembered for his style and attitude, and that is the way he wishes to be remembered generations from now. "Without sounding too corny, I'd like to be remembered as a person who built clean, detailed bikes with heart, not just for the money," Jerry says. "We have always said that if we didn't have to have money to live, we would survive off of our customers' satisfaction and compliments." You can't beat that.

So, having spent his life playing with cars and bikes, tinkering with motors, and coming home covered in oil every night, is Jerry Covington living his dream? "Most of the time I'd have to say, yes, I'm living my dream," Jerry laughs. "But sometimes it seems more like a nightmare! Seriously, not many people can say

The sun sets on a perfect day
before the Original Productions
cameras. And the crowd goes wild!
Covington family archive

Covington triumphantly raises
the trophy for the Discovery
Channel's *Biker Build-Off*. He won
against Warren Vesley from Scooter
Shooterz. *Covington family archive*

that they are doing something they love and have their family working with them. So, I believe I *am* living my dream, and that my dream will continue through my boys."

Ah yes, dreams. With four sons and a daughter to leave his custom legacy to, Jerry may rest easy. For there is no doubt that in time, there'll be another little boy or girl bent over a bicycle in a garage somewhere in Woodward, Oklahoma, creating and dreaming big dreams.

Just like grandpa Jerry, they'll be bad to the bone. ✪

VQ BIKE

OWNER: Damien Lively

YEAR OF BUILD: 2004

ENGINE: Total Performance 124-inch Evo-type

FRAME: Covington Limo

SPECIAL FEATURES: Given away in a raffle for the Broward, Florida, Boys and Girls Club at the annual VQ Ball in Daytona Beach.

HEIR TO THE CUSTOM THRONE

CORY NESS

CHAPTER 3

CORY NESS' *TRIPLE THREAT*

It's no easy task to go up against the world's most famous custom bike builder, especially when he's your father! But that's exactly what Cory Ness had to do with his first *Biker Build-Off* entry. Cory's sleek gold-plated chopper *(see page 106)* won that round and he soon found himself going up against Eric Gorges of VooDoo Choppers for round two.

For his second *Build-Off* bike, Cory pulled no punches, going all out with this amazing three-cylinder W3 motor by the late Jim Feuling which puts out over 150 horsepower! While most of this one-off wonder bike was handmade by Cory, you'll find a choice selection of parts and products that came right from the Ness catalog as well. In the end, this Triple Threat road warrior took the day and Cory rode home . . . victorious.

TRIPLE THREAT

OWNER: Cory Ness

YEAR OF BUILD: 2004

ENGINE: Feuling three-cylinder

FRAME: Ness Y2K Softail, modified by Kurt Winter

SPECIAL FEATURES: Last three-cylinder engine made by the late Jim Feuling's company prior to being sold following Feuling's death; rotated backwards 45 degrees; 150 pounds of torque.

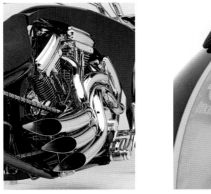

TRIPLE THREAT

Young Cory Ness—heir to the kingdom of custom bikes—at the old Ness Cycle shop in San Leandro, California. *Ness family archive*

CORY NESS

THIS CLASSIC TALE TAKES PLACE IN DUBLIN . . . DUBLIN, CALIFORNIA, THAT IS. There is a castle, there is a king, and there is his son, who is the heir of a great kingdom. There are fire-breathing dragons, though these are of the two-wheeled variety, and there is a noble goal, but more on that later.

Once upon a time, in the mythic realm of Oakland, there was a man who wielded a mighty paint gun instead of a sword. His name was Arlen Ness. As the legend goes, Arlen once went out and bought a used Knucklehead Harley-Davidson. Upon bringing the bike home, our hero was promptly yelled at by his wife, Beverly. In many such stories, the wife would say something like, "Either that damned bike goes, or I do!" Now, Beverly may have said some such thing,

Cory is ready to light up the night with this radical pavement pounder. It was the third bike he built and is now in Ness Museum. *Ness family archive*

but when the smoke cleared, both the bike and Bev stayed, as did Arlen.

Much has been written about Arlen Ness and we will not try to tell of his legendary exploits here, for this is the story of Arlen's son, Cory. Suffice it to say that Arlen and Cory have created a vast kustom kingdom and that bike builders and owners across the land have benefited from the incredible parts and products that the Ness dynasty design and market.

Cory Ness was born in Oakland on August 11, 1963, the only son of Arlen and Beverly, and brother to his sister Sherry, two years his senior. Cory grew up in a rather normal American household, save for one thing—there were motorcycle parts all over the place.

"Motorcycles were part of everyday life around our house," Cory remembers. "My dad was always custom painting a bike out in the garage and the fumes would pour out," Cory laughs. "Whenever a big bike show was coming up there would be a lot of activity to get the latest custom bike ready for the show. Dad would work on the bike right in the front room of our house. It was a very interesting scene."

When Cory was a boy, his dad would pick him up and sit him on the gas tank of one of his bikes and ride him around the neighborhood. You could say that motorcycling was in Cory's blood from the start. "But I didn't get pushed into

STRICTLY BIZ-NESS 2

83

OWNER: Cory Ness

YEAR OF BUILD: 1995

ENGINE: S&S 88-inch Evo-type

FRAME: Ness Dyna Rubber Mount

SPECIAL FEATURES: Follow up to Arlen's *Strictly Biz-Ness.*

STRICTLY BIZ-NESS 2

Three generations of Ness: Cory with youngest son Max and Zackery with Arlen in the shadows. *Ness family archive*

bikes," Cory says. "I remember that the whole bike show thing was very intriguing to me. Pretty soon I wanted to start customizing things myself and began by custom painting my bicycle at age 10. My dad's friend Jeff McCann did some gold leaf on that bike. It wasn't long before my friends wanted me to paint their bikes just for fun."

Not long after that Cory got hold of a minibike and custom painted it. It was obvious, as the old saying goes, that the nut did not fall far from the tree.

"I was 14 when I bought a Honda 360 from a neighbor. I tore it apart, flame painted it, and rode it around like that for a while," Cory says. "Then I sold it and actually made a few bucks. You could say that I saw how the business worked,

An important early build for Cory (at age 15), this digger-style bike began with a Harley-Davidson Sportster motor he bought for $800 dollars. *Ness family archive*

buy a bike, fix it up, sell it, and make money. Then when I was 15 I bought a basket case from Barry Cooney, who ran B&B Choppers at the time. I got that Sportster basket case from Barry for 800 bucks and built my first Harley."

Cory remembers that money was tight so he had to use ingenuity instead of cash to customize his bike. "We had a beadblaster in the garage, so I blasted most of the engine parts and did a little chrome. Then I found an old, beat-up and battered Sportster tank in our backyard and took it over to Bob Dron. He put a flat bottom on the tank for me. That was the look back then. The Sportster was a low-budget build but a great way to learn to customize. I got my first magazine cover with that Sportster," Cory smiles. "Then I sold it and used the money to buy my first car."

To make some extra money, Cory used to work for Arlen after school throughout high school and on the weekends. He would hand-assemble Arlen's long, custom springer front ends out in the garage.

"The business was so small when I grew up that my parents never pushed me to come into the business." But like many of today's master bike builders, the bike bug bit Cory hard. "I wanted to ride, and in my senior year I got an all black Sportster and rode it to school. My parents were concerned about my safety, as any parent would be, but they were also understanding."

Cory got into custom painting at an early age. Check out the gold leaf swirls! Named "Number One Bike in the Country" in 1981. *Ness family archive*

It's good to be King.
Father and son riding
together on bikes of their
own design. Cory was 21
years old and it was
his first ride to Sturgis.
Ness family archive

Even for the son of the
world's best-known
custom builder, the
excitement of getting
one of your bikes shot
for a motorcycle
magazine never fades.
Ness family archive

After graduating high school in 1981, Cory took college classes in business, marketing, and advertising. "I thought those classes would come in handy for the family business and our parts catalog, but the advertising classes were frustrating. It seemed like 80 percent of the time the classes were about how to make a TV commercial," Cory recalls. "So I kept on working, dug into the motorcycle business, and focused on doing our catalog."

The Arlen Ness catalog has grown by leaps and bounds under Cory's thoughtful gaze. In 1984, just a few years after Cory got out of school, Harley-Davidson came out with their Evolution engine. The Porsche-designed motor did not leak or have any of the problems that Harley's Shovelhead motor was known for. Soon, doctors, lawyers, and average Joes were buying new Harley-Davidsons. Most everyone who owns a Harley gets into customizing their bike a bit in order to make it uniquely their own. Arlen and Cory began to design new parts to fit the Evo motor at the same time that another interesting trend hit the motorcycle market.

"In 1987 we started putting out aftermarket parts made from billet aluminum," Cory says. "We started by making billet handgrips. I remember we asked ourselves why anyone would spend 80 bucks to buy billet handgrips when you could buy rubber ones for six bucks. The billet grips were not cheap

OWNER: Cory Ness

YEAR OF BUILD: 1997

ENGINE: S&S 88-inch lower end; Patrick Racing top end with handcrafted fin pattern

FRAME: Ness-Tail with five-inch stretch

SPECIAL FEATURES: Appeared in *Vanity Fair* and *Wired* magazines; only bike in Young Designers exhibit in Cooper-Hewitt National Design Museum, Smithsonian Institute.

to manufacture, but we were selling them as fast as we could make them. We discovered that people would pay for something unique. Soon, we were making everything out of aluminum, and we were the first to have billet products out there for a long time."

With the success of the Evo motor and billet aluminum custom parts, the Ness catalog began to grow, and so did the V-twin motorcycle industry. "It seemed like it took forever for us to sell $1 million a year in parts," Cory says. "But then when we got there, we snowballed right passed it and kept on going." The billet craze fueled the growth at Ness with $80 handgrips, $200 mirrors, $300 lifter blocks, and so on. Soon, the Ness catalog included nearly everything

CURVACEOUS-NESS

you need to build a bike from scratch. Today, you will find Ness wheels, brakes, frames, tanks, fenders, grips, foot controls, front ends, motors, and more, all from the company that began with just a simple pair of handlebars that Arlen made in his garage.

Likewise, the Ness castle has grown from the humble garage in Oakland to their long-time shop in San Leandro, to the massive new 68,000-square-foot facility in Dublin. Arlen and Cory moved into the new digs about two years ago. The place is a customizer's dream, offering a state-of-the art custom shop, parts warehouse, offices, showroom, custom bike museum, even room for Arlen's cool car collection. Besides creating their own line of production motorcycles under the Ness Motorcycle LLC name, they sell American IronHorse, Victory, and Big Dog motorcycles.

In fact, over the past five years Arlen and Cory have helped to completely redesign the look of Victory motorcycles, even offering a special Arlen Ness edition Victory Vegas model. They also developed a bike for American IronHorse

WEDGE

OWNER: Cory Ness

YEAR OF BUILD: 1996

ENGINE: Sputhe 105-inch Evo-type

FRAME: Ness FXR-style

SPECIAL FEATURES: Cory worked with Carl Brouhard on the sketches; first MC project by Dan Baumick, owner of Fat Kats tanks.

based on their award-winning Y2K frame. With all this big business going on, it is sometimes difficult to get back to basics and the reason this whole incredible empire began, namely, riding.

"I find that you have to ride a motorcycle and get out on the open road in order to reawaken that passion for riding," Cory says. "Riding to Sturgis, being out in the middle of nowhere, opens your mind to how to make a motorcycle better, more comfortable, cooler looking. Working in the office doesn't do that. Inspiration comes from riding."

So, riding keeps the passion alive and the whole industry real. You can see Cory's passion for riding in every sleek curve of the bikes he designs and builds. "I like nice flowing lines," Cory says. "Whether the bike is a chopper or a digger-style, or whatever, it has got to flow. One piece has to flow into the next. I never build anything that is chopped up. My bikes are always long and stretched out, clean, and functional."

To better understand what Cory is talking about, all you would have to do is look at the cover of *VQ* magazine from August 1999. I was lucky enough to be involved with *V-Twin Quarterly* at that time and remember being blown away by Cory's aptly named *Curvaceous-Ness*.

Cory originally sketched out the flowing lines of this bold, blue machine with conceptual artist Carl Brouhard. The bike began with an 88-ci Evo motor sporting

Nigel Patrick Racing cylinders that were given special treatment by Ness machinist John Ferrantino. The Ness hidden-shock frame was stretched 5 inches and the swingarm was 2 inches over stock to give the bike its long, fluid look. All the bodywork was hand-formed aluminum without one drop of Bondo.

The bike was a rolling catalog for the latest Ness products from the handlebar and foot controls to the gas tank, mirrors, and grips. Ness Tech brakes locked down on the Ness Smooth billet wheels, and the Ness billet primary was the icing on the cake. Naturally, bike builders and owners rushed out in a buying frenzy to get some of those curvaceous parts on their own scoots.

continued on page 98

TURNED LOOSE

OWNER: Arlen Ness

YEAR OF BUILD: 1985

ENGINE: 1958 Harley-Davidson XL

FRAME: Ness Lo-Liner, built by Jim Davis

SPECIAL FEATURES: Wheels Lester mags for Japanese bike; engraving by Larry Thomas, a gun engraver; paint by Cory Ness, with leafing and striping by Jeff McCann; third bike Cory built—first magazine cover bike (*Street Chopper* magazine)

TURNED LOOSE

145

OWNER: S&S

YEAR OF BUILD: 2003

ENGINE: S&S 145-inch Evo-type

FRAME: Ness Y2K

SPECIAL FEATURES: Frame modified to accept 145-inch engine and dual-belt final drive (needed to handle power of the engine); part of a project to commemorate the introduction of the 145-inch engine.

The legendary motorcycle usually sits proudly as the centerpiece of the Ness showroom; the jeweled crown of the Ness legend, so to speak. As this is being written, the curvy custom with its timeless lines is on display in the San Jose Art Museum as part of a tribute to Motorcycles as art form.

But *Curvaceous-Ness* was just the beginning for this talented builder. Over the years, Cory's customs have graced the pages of virtually every major motorcycle magazine in the world and more recently, his efforts have won him high praise on the Discovery Channel's *Biker Build-Off* series.

Unlike many of the other bike builders in this tome, Arlen and Cory Ness did not need me to introduce them to Hugh King and Thom Beers. The king and heir-apparent of the custom bike world were already well known to the *Build-Off* crew, and the ultimate episode of the show actually pitted the father and son against each other in a no-holds-barred build-off.

In the finale of that episode, Cory and Arlen shipped their show bikes to Hawaii and rode with the local bikers before the Discovery cameras. The locals voted for their favorite of the two Ness bikes and in a touching passing of the royal scepter from father to son, Cory took the day with grace and style.

Does being part of such two-wheeled TV help business? "Well, our website goes nuts!" Cory says. "TV offers us great exposure, and I feel it helps us to pave the way for a better future. Kids watch those shows and that helps foster a

Father and son, Arlen and Cory Ness, astride two throwback customs that hark back to the days of flame jobs and apehangers. Choppers are forever!
Ness family archive

Cory and Kim Ness.

whole new riding generation out there. They also buy our motorcycle toys at Wal-Mart and Toys R Us," Cory laughs. "Seriously, there is a whole new generation of riders and builders coming up, thanks to their getting excited about motorcycles from watching those shows."

When it comes to building custom bikes, Cory is quick to give credit to his talented staff of over 100 employees at Ness and the close-knit build team he and his father have put together. That team assembles around 25 one-off custom bikes per year. When asked what influences his swoopy designs, Cory remarks that he enjoys going to the European bike shows for inspiration. "I love to see the latest concept bikes and sportbikes. Plus there's great custom bike building talent out there. Guys like Roger Goldammer and Matt Hotch. Their stuff is very clean, smooth lines, my kind of stuff."

Cory Ness has been designing Ness parts for over 10 years now, and their bread and butter is not in building custom bikes, but rather in selling parts and products for everyday bikes and everyday riders. "We use custom bikes to help us launch new products, but the majority of the parts we sell are purchased by people who own a fairly stock bike by Harley-Davidson."

The entire Ness family is involved in the business. Arlen and Beverly are still at their posts everyday. Daughter Sherry acts as Arlen's assistant, and Cory and his wife Kim have two sons who are even getting into the act. Zackery is 17 and

HARD ROCK

Max is 11. Both boys have been into bikes from the first time they saw one, and that comes early at the Ness house. Zack built his first bike at age 15, and like his father before him, he sold the bike and thought that was cool. He made enough money to buy a pickup truck. "Zack built the bike himself," Cory is proud to mention. "He works at Ness on the weekends. He drew out what the bike would look like, and followed the same path that I did."

"Max has been feeling a bit left out," Cory smiles. "He's only 11 and can't build a bike yet, but I saw these cool little minichoppers at the V-Twin Expo last month, and I bought him one that is stripped down. I'm going to show him how to put it together and paint it." And so, another Ness bike builder is born.

OWNER: Cory Ness

YEAR OF BUILD: 2004

ENGINE: Feuling three-cylinder

FRAME: Ness Y2K

SPECIAL FEATURES: Built for Seminal Hard Rock
Casino and Hotel Tour; Fagnel supercharger;
24-karat gold plating.

HARD ROCK

As one of the illustrious Lucky Seven, I had to ask if Cory is living his dream. There was not a second's hesitation when he said, "I am definitely living my dream. There isn't anything else I'd rather do. Less responsibility would be nice sometimes, but being around motorcycles and working with your hands is great. I've had the opportunity to travel around the world and meet incredible people. Wherever I go, people have heard of our family. It opens doors to new friendships."

What advice would Cory give to other bike builders? "Build what you enjoy and do your own thing. If you're good at what you do, just keep perfecting your style and you will be recognized."

HAWAII BUILD-OFF BIKE

OWNER: Cory Ness

YEAR OF BUILD: 1995

ENGINE: S&S 124-inch Evo-type

FRAME: Modified Ness Y2K

SPECIAL FEATURES: Magna Charger supercharger; tank is part of frame; bodywork handcrafted by Cory and Bob Munroe.

As the sun was setting on this custom Camelot, we asked Cory how he would like to be remembered. "I'd like to be remembered as a good person who helped bring the motorcycle industry to a new level, and be known as a good family man who enjoyed bikes and had a passion for it."

That's an easy wish to grant, for you are all those things, Mr. Ness. But we will add one last sentence to this tale of castles, kings, and customs: They rode happily ever after. ✪

FANNING THE FLAMES

DAVE
PEREWITZ

CHAPTER 4

ARRIVEDERCHE

109

DAVE PEREWITZ
ARRIVEDERCHE

Putting this radical red ride together in the dead of
winter was no easy task, even for veteran builder Dave
Perewitz. This *Biker Build-Off* sled went up against
rowdy rebel Billy Lane of Melbourne, Florida. Billy won
by the slimmest of margins. Beginning with a single
downtube Rolling Thunder frame, Dave sandwiched in
a 121-cubic inch TP Engineering motor along with two
Mikuni HSR-42 carburetors and a Baker RSD tranny.
Wheels and brakes are top quality units by
Performance Machine.

Naturally, master painter Perewitz handled the
signature flame paint job himself, utilizing none other
than Mario Andretti's one-of-a-kind *Arrivederche* Red
paint. The bike was a tribute to Mario, but Dave rides
this bad boy himself.

OWNER: Frank Cotroneo

YEAR OF BUILD: 2003

ENGINE: Total Performance 121-inch Evo-type

FRAME: Perewitz/Rolling Thunder

SPECIAL FEATURES: *Arrivederche* Red color PPG mixed just for Mario Andretti's final race car and retired after last race—used with permission from Andretti; engine hand-built by Tom Pirone, owner of Total Performance; dual Mikuni carburetors; Perewitz and Ron Landers built the frame at Rolling Thunder facility in Canada; Perewitz signature flames.

DAVE PEREWITZ

LAST YEAR GIBSON GUITAR HELD A GALA EVENT DURING DAYTONA BIKEWEEK HONORING THE THREE KINGS OF CUSTOMS. Each of these three master bike builders created a ground-up custom motorcycle and a wild Gibson Guitar to match it. The fact that a large company such as Gibson picked these particular three gentlemen is a testament to the fact that all three are universally recognized as America's most famous bike builders. They were Arlen Ness, Donnie Smith, and Dave Perewitz.

These three kings, who have known each other for over 30 years, are good friends as well as being riding partners and bona fide national treasures. Despite fame and fortune, all three men are still very down-to-earth and approachable.

A long way from the road to fame and glory, but this is how it all began for Dave and many bike builders; buying and selling parts at swap meets.
Perewitz family archives

Perewitz brought the
California Digger–style
made famous by
Arlen Ness to the East
Coast. Here are two
wild examples. *Perewitz
family archives*

DAVE
PEREWITZ

113

While much has been written on Arlen and Donnie, we thought we would share
with you the true all-American story of Dave Perewitz. Because if ever there was a
man who belongs in this select grouping of the Lucky Seven, it is surely Dave. As
you will soon discover, he is a man who lives, eats, and breathes motorcycles.

Born in Brookline, Massachusetts, on February 26, 1951, Dave grew up with
a mom, a dad, and two brothers, in what he calls a traditional *Leave it to Beaver*
family. His father was an architect in marine design who enjoyed his son's love of
customizing.

"I used to build model cars as a kid," Dave remembers. "I would melt the
plastic parts with a candle to customize them. When I was 12 I even won
a trophy at the Brockton Fair for one of my models. I think it was a 1962 Ford."

An older cousin of Dave's owned a '32 Ford three-window coupe, and
the young Perewitz loved to walk down to the garage where all the older guys
were building hot rods. But soon, Dave's attention turned to custom motorcycles.
The defining moment that turned the boy from Brookline into a biker is still
etched in his mind as if it happened yesterday. "I saw a big poster in my cousin's
garage for the 1963 Flywheels Auto Club Show and I talked my father into taking
me," Dave recalls. "That's where I saw my very first custom motorcycle. It was

a Harley-Davidson Panhead that was chopped out. I remember thinking, 'This is me, a hot rod that's a motorcycle.'"

By the time Dave was 15, a friend of his had a Honda 305 Scrambler and Dave used to tear around the neighborhood on that bike. "Back then you had to have *two* license plates on a motorcycle, one in front and one in back," Dave laughs. "It looked real goofy."

At 16, Dave had become friends with a girl whose mom owned the local Harley-Davidson dealership. "She always had a new bike," Dave says. "She used to let me ride her 900 XLCH Sportster around. Then one of my best friends went to Vietnam in 1967. When he was over there he bought a bike and brought it

This is one accessory you won't find in any chopper builder's catalog. As if a Perewitz paint job wasn't enough of an attention grabber ...
Perewitz family archive

back with him. It was a '59 Sportster with a 74-cubic-inch stroker motor. He and I shared a garage together and he left that Sporty in the garage. We'd start it up every once in a while, and I'd just listen to that motor," Dave smiles. "I said, 'I gotta have one of these.' So, I sold an old car I had (Dave actually owned an car at the tender age of 12 and used to tinker with it in the back yard) and bought a 1964 XLCH, *the* bike to have at the time."

The Harley Sportster was a very fast bike in the mid-1960s, and the CH designation stood for Competition Hot. The 1964 XLCH featured a 55-ci (883-cc) kick start–only Shovelhead motor with race-inspired gear ratios in its four-speed transmission.

"That bike was the beginning for me," Dave says. I bought it for 800 bucks and began experimenting on it right away." Perewitz did a mild customizing job on the XL at first, but soon, "I cut the shit out of it," Dave laughs. "It got reduced to rubble real quick. I put a hardtail on the rear end, stretched the frame 6 inches, put a Mother's 16-over springer front end on it, a King and Queen seat, and I made the sissy bar and footpegs myself. I beat the shit outta that thing and then sold it for $2,300 back in 1971. That was a lot of money back then."

Dave Perewitz was making the transition from motorcycle enthusiast to custom bike builder and biker. A friend from Roxbury used to help Dave buy used bikes and basket cases on the cheap. "He was a biker and he'd turn me on to

OWNER: Bob Belenger

YEAR OF BUILD: 2003

ENGINE: Harley-Davidson Twin Cam with factory
95-inch kit

FRAME: Daytec Rigid

SPECIAL FEATURES: Fork a stock H-D Springer modified
so handlebars are part of the top triple clamp.

MAROON CHOP

117

guys from the ghetto who needed to sell their bikes. I'd buy them for $400 or
$500. One time we got in the van and drove all the way to the Bronx in New York
City to buy some bikes. We got three complete bikes as basket cases for like
$1,200. That was a score and a half! One of those bikes was the very first one
I ever got into a magazine."

In 1974 *Custom Chopper* magazine featured a wild custom chopper by Dave
Perewitz. "Me and my friends all used to read the chopper magazines back then.
I thought my bikes were as good as the ones in the magazines, so I called up the
editor out of the blue and told him he should put one of my bikes in his magazine. Believe it or not, he said he would be out to shoot some of my bikes in two

Dave and Suzy, early 1980s. "The business wouldn't be half what it is without her," Dave says. "She never complains, even when I'm on the road all the time." *Perewitz family archives*

An impromptu hootenanny with motorcycle artist and friend David Mann, known for his biker-lifestyle art seen in *Easyriders* magazine. *Perewitz family archives*

weeks. He came out sight unseen and shot four bikes."

By this time, Dave was becoming a biker. He got a tattoo, grew his hair long, and his *Leave it to Beaver* family took notice. "My dad was pretty cool, he didn't mind the bikes. But my mother said, 'Don't ride those bikes,' and, 'Don't get any more of those tattoos.'

"Actually, thinking back, my parents were pretty supportive. My dad has a woodworking shop in the cellar, and he used to let me mold frames down there. We also had a 4x10-foot shed out back that was full of lawnmowers, old bicycles, and stuff. Dad let me turn it into my first spray paint booth. I found an old kitchen fan, cut it into the wall, and started spraying bikes. When my parents moved in 1992, there was still metalflake paint on the floor of that shed."

Dave's life revolved around custom bikes by the late 1960s, and he remembers being mentored into the biker lifestyle by a very special friend. "What pushed me over the edge was in 1969 I was a line mechanic at a Chevy dealer and I met a guy that worked next to me," Dave recalls. "He was older and from Boston. I was just a kid from a small town, and Bobby Portnoy took me under his wing. I went from the small scene to the big scene. All we cared about was motorcycles, motorcycles, motorcycles."

Perewitz worked in a machine shop for a little while in 1970. "That was the last job I had," Dave says. It's very telling that the bike builders of our Lucky

Dave's first bike shop. Note his friendly and knowledgeable counterman, always ready to help with your every custom need. *Perewitz family archives*

This is what a chopper looked like back in the day (mid-1970s). Naturally, it had to have a Dave Perewitz paint job. *Perewitz family archives*

Dave Perewitz opened his shop Cycle Fabrications in 1975. His friend Paul Mareb came up with the name and it stuck. *Perewitz family archives*

Seven don't consider their careers *work*. They love what they do and wouldn't be doing anything else.

America had gone motorcycle crazy by the mid-1970s. The film *Easy Rider* debuted in 1969 as did the NBC television series *Then Came Bronson*. High school kids were buying motorcycles in record numbers and the first issue of *Easyriders* magazine appeared in June of 1971. Choppers were the rage, and Dave Perewitz was primed and ready to open Cycle Fabrications.

"I remember the very minute we came up with the name," Dave chuckles. "I was driving around with a couple of buddies, a 12-pack on the floor of the car (which Dave's Boston accent turns into 'cah'). I was trying to come up with a name for my custom shop and my friend Paul Mareb said, 'How about Cycle Fabrications?' I said, 'Yep, that's it!'"

Dave's father and one of his oldest friends from the neighborhood helped him build a shop on the family property. The first Cycle Fabrications building was just 12x18 feet, about the size of a one-car garage. Back in 1975, when Cycle Fabrications officially opened its doors, Dave would paint a motorcycle tank and fenders for $35 to $50. A big job that included raking and molding the frame, converting the swingarm, and painting everything including the frame and oil tank cost around $300. "In the 1970s a custom paint job might include three or four pieces, and nowadays, a custom bike might have as many as 30 pieces to paint.

Materials that were 25 bucks back then cost me over $1,000 now." It's no wonder that a one-of-a-kind Dave Perewitz paint job goes for anywhere from $2,500 to $10,000 these days.

"Back when I started building bikes there were no aftermarket motors. You had to find an old basket case, and most of the old Harley motors were pretty beat up," Dave remembers. "Then you had to find a guy who could weld aluminum, and then send the parts out to get polished. It was a major ordeal. At that time you had to modify existing bikes, not remove and replace parts."

Cycle Fabrications builds 12 to 15 custom bikes per year and all have the very distinctive Perewitz touch. Whether you happen to see a classic Perewitz

PURPLE CHOP

OWNER: Dave Perewitz

YEAR OF BUILD: 2004

ENGINE: S&S 145-inch Evo-type

FRAME: Modified Daytec Softail

SPECIAL FEATURES: Built for *Easyriders*
Centerfold Tour; Jeff Klock,
owner of TCX, hand built the pipes

The new mega-sized Cycle Fabrications building opened in 2005. Naturally, Dave held a party to end all parties. Some things never change. *Perewitz family archives*

Dave and Suzy last year at the Discovery Channel *Biker Build-Off* ride. What a long, strange trip it's been, eh, kids? *Perewitz family archives*

bobber, one of Dave's wild choppers, or a long and low pro-street Perewitz putt, all share certain design elements that add up to the Perewitz "look." "I like long, sleek, roadworthy bikes with style," Dave says. "I really concentrate on the overall lines of the bike no matter what style it is. It has to flow from front to back and have a color scheme and paint scheme that fit the style of the way the bike flows. I think it's important to follow through on the details of whatever style you are going for. And one of the most important things to me is that the bike is roadworthy. There are so many crazy-looking bikes out there today, but can you actually ride them? I don't want to build anything that I wouldn't enjoy riding."

Perewitz bikes have impeccable fit and finish. Each part flows into the next and gives the effect that the bike is hewn from one massive piece of metal that has been lovingly sculpted into a true one-off wonder, a moving sculpture. Dave's signature flame paint jobs have a unique look to them as well. In the custom world, painters and builders often refer to the look of "Perewitz flames" as a specific look they are going for. The long, scalloped flames are like Dave signing his masterpiece of moto-art and he is often referred to as the "father of flames."

After 35 years of working from 7:30 in the morning to 10 at night, this master builder is enjoying the fruits of his labors. Cycle Fab has a line of products that are sold at the distributor level. "I don't have to advertise," Dave

The Perewitz progeny and proud papa: Jodi (left) takes care of the Cycle Fab clothing line and running the retail store. Jesse (on far right) is 24 and just getting into the family business. *Perewitz family archives*

says. "I create the products and the distributor does the rest." Perewitz also has
his whole family working at the business. His longtime wife Suzy runs the office,
pays the bills, works the showroom, does the shipping, "And yells at me once in
a while," Dave laughs. "The business wouldn't be half what it is without her. She
never complains, even when I'm on the road all the time."

The kids have been involved with bikes since their births and are in the
act as well. "Jesse has been great with small engine repair since he was a kid,"
Dave says proudly. "Now at 24, he's ready to get involved with the family
business." Dave's daughter Jodi handled the Cycle Fab clothing line and running
the retail store. She also loves to ride. In fact, Jesse and Jodi are helping
Dave to build a Panhead bobber for Jodi to ride in Sturgis this year. "Jodi has a
true love of bikes," Dave confides. "She has that motorcycle passion deep in
her soul."

The biker lifestyle revolves around motorcycles, family, and friends. When
it comes to friends, Dave Perewitz counts Arlen Ness and Donnie Smith as close
brothers in arms. All three of the men have won the prestigious Lifetime
Achievement Award from *V-Twin* and *Easyriders* magazines.

"I met Arlen back in 1974 and he really helped me," Dave says. "In 1975
people were still just building choppers. I changed the East Coast scene by

building Bay Area–style customs like the ones Arlen was doing. He was the first guy out there doing West Coast diggers, and I was sort of the East Coast Ness guy."

When Dave opened his shop in 1975, Arlen was the first one to lend a hand. "He sent me a bunch of his parts to sell and said, 'Here, you need these. Pay me later.' Then he flew out to visit me later that year and we went to Laconia Bike Week together. We had only met a couple of times but he said he knew a few guys in Detroit we could go and visit." Arlen's friends turned out to be master painter Yosemite Sam, two-wheeled metal artist Ron Finch, and builder Tony Carlini.

OWNER: Ruben Brown

YEAR OF BUILD: 2003

ENGINE: Total Performance 121-inch Evo-type

FRAME: Modified Daytec Softail

SPECIAL FEATURES: Brown, an eight-time Pro Bowler, played for Buffalo Bills and Chicago Bears; one of four bikes Perewitz built for Brown, all of which are oversized to accommodate Brown's massive frame.

ORANGE CHOP

127

"We had a blast," Dave grins. "We rode our bikes, stayed at Sam's place, and you know, when you meet people on their own level, they treat you differently. Being introduced to those guys by Arlen made all the difference. I was instantly legit."

The Perewitz name has gained recognition thanks to word-of-mouth in the custom world, 35 years of motorcycle magazine coverage in *Easyriders* and others, and yes, the Discovery Channel's *Biker Build-Off* TV series. Executive Producer Hugh King met Dave Perewitz during the filming of *Motorcycle Mania*, when Jesse James and Dave rode in to the Camel Roadhouse in Daytona Beach to show off their latest custom creations. When the build-off show went from

continued on page 130

GREEN CHOP

OWNER: Brad Whitford

YEAR OF BUILD: 2003

ENGINE: Jim's 116-inch Twin Cam B

FRAME: Modified H-D Softail

SPECIAL FEATURES: Whitford guitar player in
the band Aerosmith; Whitford received
stock Softail from H-D in partial
payment for band's performance at
Harley's 100th anniversary celebration;
Jim's 116-inch engine uses stock
H-D cases—everything else is from
Jim's; Jesse James polished the engine.

GREEN CHOP

131

Would you buy used motorcycle parts from this man? Like many custom builders who have been around a while, Dave truly lived the lifestyle. *Perewitz family archives*

Dave shows us that there's a little bit of bad boy in even the nicest guys, circa 1972. *Perewitz family archives*

A radical ride for the time and a Triumph to boot. Hey, Dave, where's the gas tank? *Perewitz family archives*

a couple of TV specials to a full-blown series, Hugh asked me to hook him up with a number of bike builders, and Dave was an obvious choice.

"Oh yeah," Hugh said. "I remember Dave. He's got that great accent."

I called Dave up right away and cinched the deal. "Sure," Dave said. "I'll build them a choppah."

Now, after doing quite a bit of television, I asked Dave to comment on what it's like to be a familiar face to Americans everywhere. "Well, being on TV has boosted my popularity. It has made people aware of who I am and who all these other bike-building guys are. Now people know what we do."

What advice would Dave give to young bike builders out there? "I'd say to be successful you have to live motorcycles 24/7! Have the passion. When a new

Dave builds a lot of
bikes for NASCAR stars
and sometimes get
the chance to take a few
laps. Seen here with
Biker Build-Off friends
(left to right) Indian
Larry, Billy Lane, Dave,
and Kendall Johnson.

DAVE
PEREWITZ

guys says, 'I've been doing this for a while . . . five years. What do I have to do
to be a famous guy?' I tell them that my whole life is motorcycles. My wife has to
take vacations by herself because I travel every weekend. I'm in the shop from
7:30 in the morning to 10 at night. I think nothing of it. You have to be willing to
do that for 30 years. That's part of the game."

As with all of our Lucky Seven, Dave Perewitz is a man who is truly living
his dream. "When I'm at a bike event signing autographs and a hardcore biker
comes up and says, 'I wanna tell you, I love what you're doing.' I realize he's
a guy like me. He lives and breathes motorcycles. That makes my day. I'm just a
regular guy who loves motorcycles."

That love is still fanning Dave's flames. ✴

RED FLAME

OWNER: Danny Lasoski

YEAR OF BUILD: 2002

ENGINE: Total Performance 121-inch Evo-type

FRAME: Modified Daytec Softail

SPECIAL FEATURES: Lasoski is the 2001
championship winner in the World of Outlaws
sprint car series; like all Perewitz bikes,
Danny Gray did the seat and Keith Hanson did
the paint striping.

An early generator Shovehead with enough rake and stretch to make her sit level. Many riders used Sportster motors in their slick sleds.

THE GODFATHER OF CHOPPERS

The classic Denver's look from stem to stern. Besides the 16- to 20-inch over springer, you just had to have the pullback bars, rigid frame, cobra seat, and sissybar.

Another example of a long bike with no suspension except for the flex in the forward tubes and in the frame. Note the cool molding at the neck.

MONDO
PORRAS

CHAPTER 5

OWNER: Denver's Choppers

YEAR OF BUILD: 2004

ENGINE: Accurate Engineering Evo-type

FRAME: Diamond Chassis gooseneck rigid

SPECIAL FEATURES: Designed to replicate drag bikes of the early 1970s; wheels from an actual drag-racing car of that period; extended springer fork is the trademark of Denver's Choppers—has been the company's bread and butter since the 1960s.

DIGGER

MONDO PORRAS' *DENVER'S DIGGER*

Known for his long and lean 1970s-era choppers, this *Biker Build-Off* Digger was a change of
pace for Mondo, who competed against the late, great Indian Larry. Reminiscent of the California
Bay–area Digger style made famous by Arlen Ness and Ron Simms, the bright-red rigid sports
a frame by Erwin Graham of Diamond Chassis, and Denver's own popular springer front end and
handmade gas tank. Berry Wardlow oversaw the building of the Accurate Engineering 88-cubic
inch Panhead motor, Bert Baker sent a bulletproof transmission, and John Ventriglia offered
Mondo a Primo belt drive for this rad roadrunner.

    The 12-spoke American Mag wheels are original units from the 1970s and came off an old
Denver's Chopper. Custom Controls handled the minimalist handlebars and Omar the painter
stepped in at the last minute to add a shiny cloak of righteous red paint. Special thanks go to
the Denver's crew and prayers go out to the memory of Indian Larry who died before this episode
of *Build-Off* was finished.

    Ride forever, brother.

MONDO
PORRAS

DIGGER

Back from the test ride, Mondo puts his stamp of approval on another wicked long bike.

MONDO PORRAS

NO BOOK ABOUT CUSTOM MOTORCYCLES AND THOSE WHO BUILD THEM WOULD BE COMPLETE WITHOUT A CHAPTER ABOUT DENVER MULLINS AND MONDO PORRAS. If you have ever admired a classic chopper with its long springer front end, rigid frame, pull back bars, and upswept pipes, you have Denver and Mondo to thank. These men gave birth to the California chopper style that is so popular today and the basic look of a Denver's chopper hasn't changed much since they opened shop back in 1967.

Picture five-year-old Mondo Porras packed into the family car on the long drive from his birthplace in El Paso, Texas, to the arid desert of San Bernardino, California. Little did he realize that the move would mean that his life would take

Butch "Scrap Iron" Ariza, was the master motor builder at Denver's back in the bad ol' days. Butch is still riding and raising hell. *Denver's Choppers archives*

a very different turn. Who is to say what kind of life Mondo would have had if his family had stayed in Texas? But even as a kid, Mondo wasn't the type to look back, and sunny California was calling.

Berdoo, as the area is fondly called, was a vast wasteland back in 1953 when young Mondo arrived. It was a small town on the verge of becoming famous for being the hometown of the Berdoo Hells Angels and other outlaw motorcycle clubs. Mondo remembers seeing his first chopped Harley-Davidson at the tender age of seven. Seven years old . . . Lucky Seven . . . another coincidence?

"I remember the first time I saw a Harley bobber bike as if it were yesterday," Mondo smiles. "I was at JB's corner market in my neighborhood. I was seven years old. A group of Road Rebels came roaring up to the store and I remember starring at the big bikers and their bikes. I knew right then that I wanted to be a biker."

I believe that most bikers and motorcycle builders have a similar experience somewhere in their early lives. I certainly recall the first custom hog I ever saw. It was black and very loud. The sensation of the noise of that Harley Panhead's straight pipes was unlike anything I had ever experienced. The throbbing pulse of that big twin seemed to be in sync with the beating of my young heart. You could call it a "defining moment." I was hooked.

Not an unusual sight back in the 1970's. Two long bikes running and one broke down. If you rode a custom bike back then, you better be able to wrench.
Denver's Choppers archives

"The places I have seen and the people I have met, and the things we used to get away with as young bikers cannot be matched today. I have lived the lifestyle all these young bikers can only read and dream about."

For Mondo, the wish to become a biker led him to buying a used Harley-Davidson Panhead during the summer after he graduated high school. "I sold my Model A Ford to get the money for the bike," Mondo remembers. "Denver took me over to one of the Hells Angels' houses and I bought the bike for $900. Man, was it nice."

Throwing a leg over your first big twin Harley can be a bit big scary. You can't help being a bit nervous about getting a big FL home in one piece. "I remember Denver saying, 'You bought it, you ride it!' I kicked that Panhead over, and I've never looked back since."

Riding became the center of Mondo's life. He and his bike became fused like a modern centaur on two wheels. "I still ride as much as I can," Mondo told us. "I built myself an FXR clone bike with a raced-up twin cam engine a little over a year ago. It is basic black. I rode it cross-country last summer to get to the *Biker Build-Off* with Indian Larry. I often ride with DJ, one of the guys who works for me. He's a Hells Angel and one of the best riders I have ever ridden with. I love riding with him and would ride to the gates of hell with him."

It is often difficult for parents to see their kids grow up and become rebellious, and Mondo's straight-laced mom and dad had little influence on the hell-raiser in their family. "My parents did not like the bike at all but I was already living on my own and raising hell," Mondo says. "The Vietnam War was in full

Mondo burns up some desert, road testing a new Denver's Chopper.

Little Freddy Hernandez proves that you can turn a 50-over springer front end around in the street. Freddy built many of the Denver's frames. *Denver's Choppers archives*

The business end of a
Denver's springer. "I love
this digger style," Mondo
says. "It takes me back to
the old days."

TRACTOR SEAT

OWNER: Charlie Baxter

YEAR OF BUILD: 2001

ENGINE: 1962 102-cubic inch Harley-Davidson Panhead

FRAME: Diamond Chassis

SPECIAL FEATURES: Mountain bike shock under tractor seat; everything handmade; built to be different: "If you don't dare to be different in this business, you melt into the background."

The word "mischievous" comes to mind. Mondo Bondo in the wild old days, circa 1971. *Denver's Choppers archives*

An early Denver's Chopper. It may look a little wobbly, but these bikes track true and run like raped apes.
Denver's Choppers archives

swing, and the biker and hippie era was going strong. I was already gaining a reputation as Bondo Mondo the custom frame molder at Denver's Choppers."

Interestingly, Mondo was the only member of his family to get bitten by the custom bike bug. "I have three brothers and one sister and they are all white collar workers," Mondo laughs. "Here's the breakdown: corporate lawyer, orthopedic surgeon, and computer programmer in the aerospace industry. My sister is the head floor nurse at Loma Linda Hospital. I guess I'm the black sheep in the family, but I am doing what I love and don't have to wear a tie to work. Oh, and come to think of it, I haven't seen *them* in books, magazines, or on the Discovery Channel."

When you became a biker back in the 1960s, you often found yourself with a new family of biker brothers. You would ride together, party together, live the lifestyle, and even die for each other if need be. "I guess I got a passion for motorcycles when it became my life and lifestyle," Mondo recalls. "Nothing else meant more to me than my family and biker brothers. I remember my wife climbing over my Knucklehead that I was building in the bedroom of our apartment. We didn't have a garage there. Oh, and by the way, she was pregnant at the time." Mondo grins.

By the late 1960s, Southern California had become the hub of the custom world. Wild hot rod cars and cool choppers were all the rage and Mondo was

OWNER: Pee Wee

YEAR OF BUILD: 1998

ENGINE: S&S 113-inch Evo-type built by Pat Mathers

FRAME: Chopper Guys FXR-style

SPECIAL FEATURES: Pee Wee, president of Hell's Angels Las Vegas chapter; bike oversized to accommodate the six-foot-six-inch-tall, 450-pound owner

right smack dab in the middle of the scene. "I started building custom bikes with Denver back in 1967. Denver was a very well known custom car painter and builder on the Southern California circuit. At the time I was learning how to do body work and custom paint on cars, so the transition to motorcycles was easy."

At that time, Denver and Mondo were experimenting with motorcycles in a way that had never been done before. Some very long bikes were coming out of the small shop in Berdoo. Springer front ends became longer and longer, as Denver continued to innovate rather than imitate.

"Denver Mullins was a one-of-a-kind guy; they don't make them like him anymore," Mondo says. "He was a true innovator, no matter what he put his mind to. He was an award-winning custom painter in the 1960s. He was installing hydraulic lifts and chopping car tops before most of your readers were even born. The whole custom motorcycle industry owes a debt of gratitude to Denver for starting the aftermarket business. We are all making a good living today thanks to guys like Denver. He was a true pioneer with a great vision for what was cool in choppers."

Mullins was also instrumental in the development of the drag boat safety capsule used by all drag boat racers today. Drag boat racing was a passion for Denver, and unfortunately led to his untimely demise. On October 4, 1992, Denver's top fuel boat crashed and sank during a test run on Southern

PEE WEE'S BIKE

149

PEE WEE'S BIKE

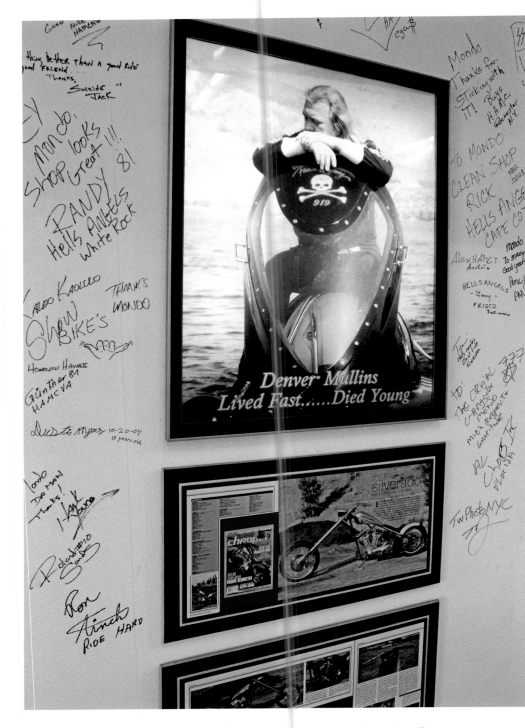

Denver Mullins
Lived Fast.......Died Young

The Godfather with one of his children—the springer front end that has become synonymous with the Denver's look.

A tribute to Denver Mullins seen on the autograph wall at the shop. Bike builders and riders from all over the world stop by to pay their respects.

California's Puddingstone Lake. The safety capsule worked, but Denver apparently panicked, trying to leave the submerged capsule, and got trapped in the process before divers could get to him. He drowned and left the custom world with a sizable hole in it.

"Denver was a great friend to all the people around him," Mondo says. "He had a great following worldwide before the advent of the TV motorcycle builder. People could look at his custom bikes going down the road and really say, 'There goes another Denver bike.' His style was often copied but never matched. He will always be Number One.

"I bought Denver's Choppers in October 1992 just after Denver was killed

Denver Mullins and Mondo in the original Denver's shop, early 1970's. Looks like every day was a party. *Denver's Choppers archives*

in our top fuel drag boat. I also bought the Drag Boat Shop. I stayed in Berdoo for a couple of years and finished all of Denver's boat and bike projects. By that time I needed a break. It was a hard couple of years. I decided to move the shop to Lake Havasu City, Arizona, and play with the drag boats for a while. I built the capsules the racers sit in with the roll cages and F16 windshields. Most everyone who raced in the pro classes used my capsule. I always kept a couple of choppers around and worked on them in my spare time. After about three years in Havasu, I decided to pick up and move the shop once again, this time to Las Vegas, Nevada. I've been here ever since. So, I guess you could say, I never really closed Denver's Choppers."

It was just after Mondo opened the new shop in Henderson, just outside Vegas, that his choppers caught the attention of motorcycle magazines once again. Choppers never really went out of style, but during the late 1980s and early 1990s, most custom bike builders were creating what have become known as billet barges. These Harley Softail–inspired bikes were all the rage until magazines like *Easyriders* turned their attention back to the long bikes that inspired many of us to ride as teenagers.

The April 2000 issue of *Easyriders* announced that Denver's Choppers was back in an articled entitled, "The Legend Lives." Here were images of classic long bikes sporting 16-inch-over springer front ends. Some had old Harley

The real thing. This is what a Denver's Chopper looked like in the 1970's, and thanks to Mondo and his crew, they still look a lot like this today. *Denver's Choppers archives*

Knuckle and Panhead engines, others used the latest Harley Evo motors. As Mondo said in the article, "Denver borrowed $120 to pay for the first month's rent to open the shop in San Bernardino (in 1967) and he never looked back."

The articled also mentioned that Little Freddie Hernandez, who started out with Mondo and Denver back in the 1960s, still supplied Denver's Choppers with the rigid chopper frames that Denver's is known for.

Right after that article ran, Mondo found an old Denver's chopper that he had helped build in 1971. I had been looking for an interesting hook for our upcoming June 2001 issue of *Easyriders* marking our 30th anniversary of publishing the biker's bible of motorcycle magazines. I talked to Mondo about

OWNER: Kenny Kuykendall

YEAR OF BUILD: 2005

ENGINE: S&S 113-inch Evo-type

FRAME: Diamond Chassis

SPECIAL FEATURES: Owner wanted hydraulic front fork instead of trademark Denver's Springer; Mondo's "yuppie bike."

MONDO PORRAS

KENNY'S BIKE

building a new chopper using the latest technology but with the classic Denver's look. We would showcase the old chop from 1971 alongside the new one from 2001 to show the world 30 years of Denver's Choppers and 30 years of *Easyriders*. I had the late David Mann, a world-famous motorcycle lifestyle artist, create a painting of the two bikes blasting down a stretch of desert road side by side as a centerspread and as the image that would launch the magazine into another 30 years.

In the opening to that article, "Hail to the Chopper," I wrote, "Together, these bikes speak volumes about why we all started riding motorcycles in the first place." Of all the bike builders on the planet, only Mondo of Denver's Choppers

KENNY'S BIKE

Mondo still builds choppers the old school way, piece by piece and all by hand.

Take a close look at this old school chop job. See anything unusual? That's not an extended springer front end, nor is it a telescopic wide glide. In fact, there is NO suspension on this puppy at all.
Denver's Choppers archives

A true chopper of the 1970's, complete with molded neck and tank. Note the similarities in the Discovery Channel *Build-Off* Digger's handlebars. This was Mondo's personal bike. *Denver's Choppers archives*

An early extended springer Panhead chop with no rake in the neck. You had to stand on your tippy-toes to ride this one.
Denver's Choppers archives

has the history and class it takes to have pulled this once-in-a-lifetime tribute off.

Unlike most bike builders, who have been influenced by other master builders, Mondo had few people around to emulate back in the day, except for Denver himself. "Other than Denver, there was really no one around to copy when I started building bikes. We designed our long bikes with long springer front ends and clean, smooth lines. I still try to do a lot of that today."

When asked to define his style of bike, Mondo told us, "The bikes I build vary from old school choppers to new-age wide-tire Softail-style bikes. I don't like to stick to any one style. My favorite bike is an FXR clone bike. It's my hot rod. I have always had a need for speed, I guess that's why I loved to build and race drag boats."

Mondo believes that Denver's Choppers hasn't really changed all that much from the shop it was in the 1960s. The biggest change in the motorcycle industry according to him, is the fact that today a builder can get everything they need to build a bike right out of an aftermarket catalog. "The fact that everyone can now buy custom made parts, assemble them, and then call themselves bike builders is beyond me," he laughs.

While Denver's only builds 8 to 10 handcrafted choppers per year, Mondo sells a lot of his unique springer front ends and rolling chassis to builders all over the world. "What I hate most," Mondo adds, "are the wannabes who copy

continued on page 164

MONDO PORRAS

159

PRO STREET

OWNER: Mondo Porras

YEAR OF BUILD: 1999

ENGINE: Highly-modified 1947 Harley-Davidson Knuckle

FRAME: Diamond Chassis

SPECIAL FEATURES: Weber two-barrel downdraft carbs; narrowed Fat Bob tanks; cross between chopper and pro-street style.

OWNER: Charlie Baxter

YEAR OF BUILD: 1971/2000

ENGINE: 1963 Harley-Davidson Panhead

FRAME: Denver's Choppers hardtail

SPECIAL FEATURES: Originally built by Denver in 1971; found by Mondo and rebuilt in 2000; orange-and-blue paint Denver's trademark colors; featured in a Dave Mann painting.

MONDO
PORRAS

LEGACY

our springers. Most of those guys can't even form an original thought, let alone their own production idea."

With that in mind, we asked Mondo to comment on his advice to other builders. "Be true to yourself and use your own style. The way to get noticed is to be original. Fit and finish is everything in a motorcycle. Make all your lines flow. Don't mix a lot of geometrical shapes. Less can be more—don't use busy paint jobs. Make the motorcycle rider-friendly. Don't lose sight of what a motorcycle is intended for."

In the past few years chopper mania has reached a fever pitch, and shows such as the *Biker Build-Off* series have helped the careers of many builders. When Hugh King was looking for bike builders with the ability to build a chopper from scratch in just 10 days, I suggested Mondo. Hugh knew of Mondo from the filming of *Motorcycle Mania II,* in which Jesse James and his road dogs stop by and visit Denver's on their way to the Sturgis Rally.

Mondo accepted the TV challenge and was paired up against Indian Larry. Just as the filming was finished, Larry died when he fell off his motorcycle during a stunt before a live audience. "The *Biker Build-Off* show meant a lot to me because it told a story of two bike builders who were lost in the prime of their lives and will never be forgotten for their contribution to us all," Mondo says.

DJ, who builds choppers
with Mondo at Denver's,
finds a use for a stock
Harley-Davidson—namely,
going fast!
Denver's Choppers archives

Blasting through the
desert near his shop in
Henderson, Nevada,
Mondo test rides a new
Denver's Chopper.

Denver, working on one of
the first choppers sporting
an early Evo motor, mid-
1980's. *Denver's Choppers
archives*

"The bikes and the ride were secondary in their build-off and that's okay with me. What I think I accomplished in the show is its own reward. I told the *Reader's Digest* version of Denver Mullins' life and the contribution he has made to the industry. If I received nothing more than that, at least people don't think we are from Denver, Colorado, anymore and that's okay by me."

As you can tell from Mondo's passion for the biker lifestyle, he is a man who is truly living his dream. "These are the best days of my life. Right now I'm just a few days away from my 56th birthday, I love my age and would not change it for anything. The places I have seen and the people I have met, and the things we used to get away with as young bikers cannot be matched today. I have lived the lifestyle all these young bikers can only read and dream about. We old guys blazed the trail so these young guys can act cool today. I am truly blessed."

How would this charter member of the Lucky Seven like to be remembered? "I'd like to be remembered as a good bike builder who cared and believed in the biker world and the people in it. That I was loyal to my friends and thankful to all the people who believed in me and helped me achieve my dreams. I could not have done it without them."

If there is a biker heaven, Denver Mullins is looking down at his old friend, brother, and partner, and you can bet he's smiling. ✺

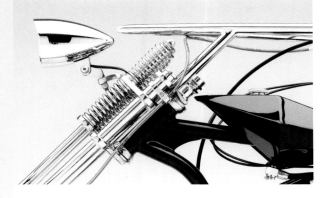

MONDO PORRAS

JAPAN BIKE

OWNER: Josh Dien

YEAR OF BUILD: 2005

ENGINE: Accurate Engineering 103-inch Panhead-type

FRAME: Diamond Chassis

SPECIAL FEATURES: Built as a Japanese-style custom; owner is five feet tall, so seat is lowered and handlebar extended; oil tank in rear fender.

MONDO
PORRAS

JAPAN BIKE

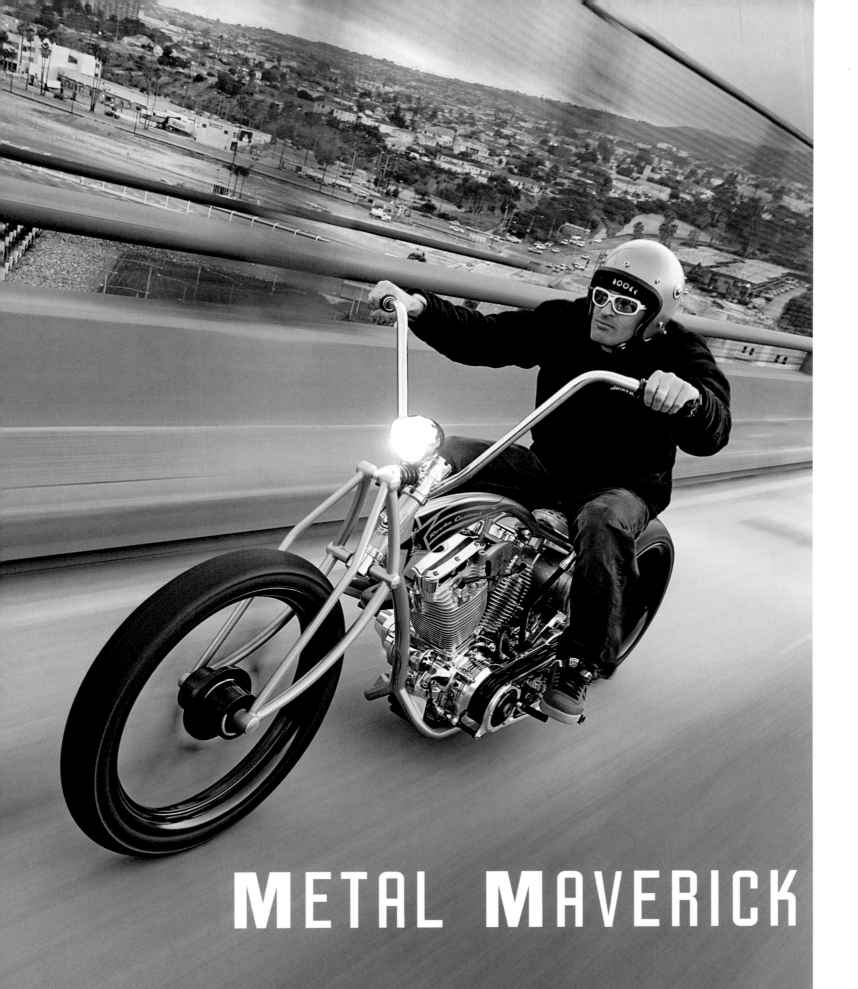

JESSE
ROOKE

METAL MAVERICK

CHAPTER 6

JESSE ROOKE'S *ROCKSTAR*

Jesse wanted to show that building a truly one-off motorcycle could be done in ten days, with time to spare, in a *Biker Build-Off* against legendary moto artist, Ron Finch of Michigan. He began by building a unique single-sided swingarm, single-downtube frame with the help of his friends, the Foddrill family, at their shop. He chose a tried-and-true S&S Cycle 96-cubic inch motor, dual Wimmer velocity stacks, Baker RSD, and Performance Machine mid-controls, as well as the prototype of their new primary drive. The girder-style front end, handlebars, tanks, wheels, and everything else are pure Rooke.

Special thanks go out to all the industry friends who have supported Jesse right from the start: James Simonelli at S&S; Bert Baker; Lee Chaffin at Mikuni; Lee Wimmer, Roland, Ted, and Perry Sands at P.M.; the Foddrill family; and Rockstar Energy Drink.

JESSE
ROOKE

ROCKSTAR

173

JESSE
ROOKE

ROCKSTAR

OWNER: Rockstar Energy Drink

YEAR OF BUILD: 2004

ENGINE: S&S 96-inch Evo-type

FRAME: Jesse Rooke Kali Kruiser

SPECIAL FEATURES: Single-sided tail section holds oil tank; gas tank under seat where oil tank normally resides; uses technology adopted from racing; number "16" refers to 16-oz size of Rockstar cans.

The need for speed started early for Jesse Rooke, here seen racing BMX bikes as a wee pup. *Rooke family archive*

JESSE ROOKE

SOME OF THE CUSTOM BIKE BUILDERS IN THIS BOOK DISCOVERED THEIR LOVE FOR MOTORCYCLES AT AN EARLY AGE. They may have seen a loud chopper roar down the street or were inspired by films like *The Wild One* or *Easy Rider*. Others were born with motorcycle oil pumping in their veins. Such a man is Jesse Rooke. Born amid the arid plains of Phoenix, Arizona, he grew up in a family of motorcyclists and attended his first motorcycle race with his parents when he was only six weeks old.

"My father was into motorcycles and racing his whole life. He had race bikes that he built and rebuilt," Jesse says. "My family didn't have much money so we had to jury rig everything on dad's bikes when something broke or got smashed.

You learn to be very innovative when you have to make parts out of old soup cans." Jesse's mother was into bikes as well. "She says that she can do wheelies but I've never seen her do it."

This gallant gearhead began riding early, borrowing his older brother's 50-cc Indian and giving his younger sister rides around the house at the tender age of three. "My parents instilled a love for bikes in me. It's really in my blood," Jesse smiles. "I've always been into bikes. The people I like are all into bikes and racer Kenny Roberts was an idol for me early on. From dirt bikes to cruisers, road racers to customs, I'm into it all. Pops had a Harley trike, which he crashed and tore himself up pretty good. That was the first Harley I remember seeing."

Even as a kid growing up, Jesse knew that he could make anything with wheels go faster by redesigning them. "I was into skateboards and BMX bicycles as a kid. I'd customize them and make them cool, add trick different color wheels, grip tape, make 'em my own."

Jesse Rooke doing what he loves best—riding on one of his cool custom creations.

Jesse's family includes two brothers and a sister. His older brother, RJ, is a top ranked bicycle racer and his younger brother, James, is into CART racing. "James was my mechanic for years when I was racing. He has been into a lot of

MARGI

OWNER: Jesse Rooke

YEAR OF BUILD: 2004

ENGINE: Kendall Johnson-built S&S 124-inch Evo-type with Stage 3 modifications

FRAME: Jesse James Dominator

SPECIAL FEATURES: Jesse James gave Jesse Rooke a frame with the stipulation he not alter it, which made this Rooke's most difficult bike to build because he had to work around the shapes James built into the frame; hand-crafted gas and oil tanks molded into the frame.

JESSE ROOKE

MARGI

179

"When you see a bike, sit on it, ride it, you get an emotion from it. That's why I build them."

Many of Jesse's innovative
ideas for custom bikes
began years before they
became a reality and were
bred on the race track.
Rooke family archive

Jesse and his dad discuss
tuning that carb one more
time. *Rooke family archive*

Kart racing was a big thrill
for young Mr. Rooke. "My
brother James was my
mechanic for years," Jesse
says. *Rooke family archive*

the same things I'm into," Jesse says. "CART racing, go-carts, dirt bikes, stuff
like that." Jesse's sister Elizabeth is the proud mother of two. "We keep her
away from the bikes, because she has crashed everything we put her on. She's
a great mom, though."

Though Jesse grew up around motorcycles of all kinds, there was a time
when his parents forbid him from riding. "Yeah, I crashed a dirt bike pretty bad
when I was 15," Jesse remembers. "My leg was broken really badly and I was
in the hospital for a long time. I had rods in my leg and my folks knew that if
I crashed another bike I'd lose my leg for sure. So I was off bikes for awhile."

Then in 2002 something happened that changed young Jesse's life
forever. "I was watching *Motorcycle Mania* on the Discovery Channel in January
2002," Jesse told us. "I was fascinated watching Jesse James make a frame
from scratch. He heated up some tubing and started bending it, and I thought,
'I could do that.'"

Rooke began building his first custom motorcycle right after seeing
Motorcycle Mania. He has Jesse James to thank for lighting the spark that has
grown into a wildfire of new motorcycle designs. "I saw *Motorcycle Mania* in
January and was building my first custom in April. It took four months to get my
first bike done," Jesse laughs. "I built that bike for me, not anybody else. I had
no plans of building bikes for a living." Then Jesse took the revolutionary

You can't take the racer out
of the kid. Jesse and two
wheels became synonymous.
Rooke family archive

Young Jesse riding high at an early age, goofing around with his dad, 1978. *Rooke family archive*

custom to the famous Del Mar Races and Bike Show and was instantly a big hit. "Everybody was so cool to me. I went to Del Mar and some good people got behind me right away."

That first custom bike was named *Dinah*. Jesse names all of his motorcycles after women and *Dinah* was, and is, still his favorite. The classy blue wonder features unique single-sided front and back wheels that makes the motorcycle look like it's floating on two wheels with no visible means of support from the right side. Jesse's inspiration came from the world of BMX bicycles and dirt bikes. "Everything I do is designed to make the motorcycle go faster. It's the racer in me," Jesse says.

Dinah was a sensation that stood the custom bike world on its ear. This 20-something designer appeared out of thin air and rocked the conventional look of customs. With the success of *Dinah*, Jesse traveled to more bike shows, runs,

Older brother RJ was
always into bikes. Here,
little Jesse hopes to
grow up just like his bro'.
Rooke family archive

Teenaged Jesse making laps on his faithful
number 66 racer. *Rooke family archive*

and events. "I went to Sturgis and fell in love with the lifestyle. I hung out with bike builder Jim Nasi and met some really cool people. I mean, I just showed up and everybody was really nice," Jesse recalls. "A security guard let me sleep at his place so I had a place to crash. I did some photo shoots for motorcycle magazines, met all the big name bike builders, Arlen Ness, Dave Perewitz. From then on it has been nonstop. Everyone in the industry has been very supportive of me."

Yet some bike builders and industry insiders scoffed at Jesse's designs, calling him the kid who builds motorcycles that look like Schwinn bicycles and calling his bikes unrideable. "I've never owned a Schwinn bike, "Jesse laughs. "I like simple dirt bikes and BMX-style bikes. My designs come from racing technology, and I guarantee that my frames are built stronger than most of the frames out there. Some people say that my bikes don't run, or they're show bikes, but I build them to ride. I like to hop on a fun bike and ride. Every bike I build conjures up a different emotion. When you see a bike, sit on it, ride it, you get an emotion from it. That's why I build them."

The dozen or so customs that followed *Dinah* are as unique and individual as Jesse is himself. There's *Phyllis*, *Cathy*, *Angel*, *Vanessa*, *Patee*, and *Margi*, as well as special industry bikes built for the Hardrock Roadhouse Tour, S&S Cycles, Dunlop tires, and one very special ride that he built with the man who lit the

Proof that chicks dig bikes. Jesse's boyish good looks don't hurt either.

spark under Rooke's butt, Mr. Jesse James. You could definitely say that all of Jesse Rooke's dreams are coming true, despite the naysayers out there.

As with all innovators, Jesse has run into his fair share of mechanics, technicians, and bike builders who have told him that something he was designing could not be done. "I just do it myself and prove to them that it can be done," Jesse says. Once he had to take apart a CNC machine so that his one-of-a-kind wheel design would fit inside the machine, and Jesse often makes the prototypes for the parts he produces just to prove to disbelievers that they can be done. He was told by machinists that his unique hidden rotor/sprocket rear brake setup could not be made. Jesse is never afraid to ask "What if . . ." and designed and built the prototype himself.

But where does Rooke's inspiration come from? "All my bikes are a representation of the influences I have grown up with: the music I listen to, the bikes I ride, my racing influences. I build a bike that is much like a race bike. I try to make them faster and better. I make them simple but cool. My Dad had bailing wire all over his bikes. I always try to make a bike look good and clean. I hide all the wires and switches and hoses. Right now, I feel like this is what I do well, I design stuff. I didn't take any design courses in school. When I was in school everybody was into becoming a doctor or a lawyer and I wasn't into that. I feel that I am finally getting to express myself through my bikes. Most people seem

RED GIRDER

OWNER: Jesse Rooke

YEAR OF BUILD: 2005

ENGINE: Kendall Johnson-built S&S
93-inch Shovel

FRAME: Jesse Rooke Kali Kruiser

SPECIAL FEATURES: Built for Seminal Hard Rock
Casino and Hotel Tour; Sweepstakes
bike—someone can win it at the end of the tour;
tank below seat segmented to hold gas in one
half and oil in the other because of the small
gas tank; most open bike Jesse has ever built.

to like what I design. Basically, I just like to experiment and make things work."

When asked to name bike builders who have influenced his designs, Jesse is hesitant to name names at first. "When I started building *Dinah*, I kept away from bike shows on purpose, because I didn't want to be influenced by anyone else's designs." Yet there are those who have helped Jesse on the journey to find his dreams. "Jesse James was a big influence. When I look at his bikes I think they're like race cars, functional and cool at the same time. The first custom bike I ever saw that I wanted to own was built by Jim Nasi, but I couldn't afford it. I like his fit and finish, his use of cool sheet metal. I dig the simplicity of Indian Larry's bikes. I think Paul Cox and Keino are doing some amazing bikes that Larry

RED GIRDER

would have been proud of. Billy Lane's brother, Warren, just built a wild bike. That thing is just crazy. Warren was one of the first people I met in the industry and he was cool to me. I also really like Roland Sands bikes. He's doing some innovative, race-inspired designs, and I like Russell Mitchell from Exile Cycles' clean, flat black bikes. I believe that as a designer, you get something from every bike you see."

With the success of *Dinah*, Jesse began his second bike in November 2003. He opened a small shop to build bikes in, but it is not open to the public. "I basically find the people that want me to build a bike for them. I only build 10 bikes per year and I have been very lucky. I find the customer, meet with them, talk with them, and see what they're into. If I like the guy and like what he's thinking, I build him a bike. But the bikes I build are 90 percent what I want to do. I don't mind taking suggestions from the customer, but they know what I'm about before I build for them," Jesse says. "I like to build what's inside my head and not be limited or restrained. I mean, people give me shit about my bikes, saying they're too far out there but look at Ron Finch's bikes. He was doing wild, off-the-wall stuff over 30 years ago." And that, my friends, is what makes Jesse Rooke an artist with metal and imagination: he innovates while others copy.

Naturally, everyone can't afford one of Jesse's lithe and agile race-inspired customs, and young Mr. Rooke remembers all too well growing up in a riding

OWNER: Jesse Rooke

YEAR OF BUILD: 2005

ENGINE: Jim's Twin-Cam 120

FRAME: Jesse Rooke Kali Racer

SPECIAL FEATURES: Built with the guys from Exile Cycle at their shop for the show *Build or Bust* after contestant was unable to finish the bike; prototype Jim's right-side-drive transmission; 9-1/2-inch rear wheel with 8-inch offset and radiuses edges.

family that used bailing wire to keep their bikes running. "I want to design and build products that the average guy can afford. Right now I'm doing front ends. I have a springer-style with billet uppers and lowers and no bolts showing anywhere. I also have the Nanna (named after banana-style bicycles), which is a girder-style front end in stock lengths. I'm making gas caps (incorporating Jesse's signature chess piece design), risers, wheels, frames, and exhaust systems. Parts are available straight through me by visiting www.rookecustoms.com, and I'm working on a line of products that will be available through Drag Specialties. I'm also working on some parts and accessories for Harley-Davidson. You'll see a lot of new stuff coming from me soon."

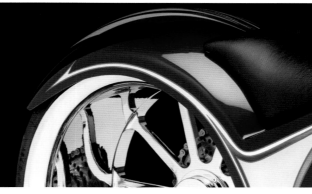

As a proud member of our Lucky Seven, Jesse Rooke is living his dream to the fullest. "Oh yeah, there's no question about it. There's been a lot of luck involved and a lot of hard work too. But I'm single and don't mind working around the clock," Jesse told us. "When it comes to the custom motorcycle industry, it's a small world and everybody knows everybody. I ask a lot of questions and I was at the right place at the right time. When I was asked to ride with the 24 top bike builders in the Discovery Channel's *Biker Build-Off* finale, it gave me chills to be with that group and ride with them. There I was riding with Arlen Ness, Eddie Trotta, Russell Mitchell, Billy Lane . . . it was so cool. I even had the chance to ride with Indian Larry at Sturgis, and tried to keep up with him."

DINAH

OWNER: Jesse Rooke

YEAR OF BUILD: 2002

ENGINE: Merch 120-inch Evo-type

FRAME: Jesse Rooke custom fabrication

SPECIAL FEATURES: Rooke's first bike—inspired by watching Jesse James on Discovery Channel; Foderill Fabrication Off-Road shock in fork; oil tank in front downtube; used left-side-drive transmission because Rooke didn't yet know he should use a right-side-drive tranny with a wide tire.

JESSE
ROOKE

DINAH

Speaking of the *Biker Build-Off* series, we asked Jesse how television and motorcycle magazine coverage has changed his life. "Being on the *Biker Build-Off* show has allowed me to build what I want to build. Customers always want to put in their two cents, but I'm trying to find myself and build crazy things. I don't have any boundaries. The TV stuff lets me have free will to build what I want. I went to Wal-Mart the other day and two people recognized me. I thought, 'Whoa, I have a lot of new friends.'

"It's crazy, my neighbors used to think I was a drug dealer because I have nice stuff, cars, boats, etc. This Girl Scout showed up on my doorstep and said, 'My mom says you're a drug dealer.' I invited them in and showed them my bikes.

Now they've seen me on TV and realize I'm just a bike builder. Thanks to TV exposure and magazine articles, my phone rings off the hook all the time. It's both a blessing and a curse. Don't get me wrong, I appreciate everything that's happening. I was racing my whole life and I like the fans. I appreciate them and hang out with them."

Of Jesse's fans, his father tops the list. "My dad is so happy about what I'm doing. His whole life has been about motorcycles, and now he sees my face in a bike magazines and he's just blown away. I feel that the industry has opened its arms to me and now I hope that I can help some young builders out there, open doors for them and help them live *their* dreams. Plus, you know, I'm making

DUNLOP

OWNER: Woody Woodford

YEAR OF BUILD: 2004

ENGINE: Kendall Johnson-built Revtech 110-inch Evo-type

FRAME: Jesse Rooke Kali Kruiser

SPECIAL FEATURES: Rear brake caliper built into frame—grabs sprocket that doubles as a brake disk.

a living at this, and it isn't easy by any means. I had no money and no budget when I built my first bikes."

But what Jesse lacked in funds he made up for with ingenuity. "I've had great success and I want to be the best and be at the top. People say that my bikes look like you can't ride them, but when you ride one you see what I'm about. You can jump my bikes; they're fun to ride. I can go out in my garage, pick a bike, and ride. That's what it's all about."

All right, all you aspiring young custom bike builders out there, Jesse Rooke has been where you are right now and he has the following advice. "Keep your head screwed on straight. Get an education, ask questions, and take the advice of experts. When you do that, builders treat you right. Focus on what you want to do and go for it. A million people have told me that I couldn't build something a certain way, so I'll go and make it. Don't dream about it—do it. I'd rather get it done and move on."

Speaking of moving on, though still at the beginning of his career, we asked Jesse how he would like to be remembered in the hallowed halls of bikerdom. "I'd like to model myself after the great builders in this book. That's the ultimate for me. I hope I'll get to work with some of them, because I love to work with people and learn their craft. I feel very blessed to be doing what I'm doing. I have the passion for what I do and I love it." ✪

JESSE ROOKE

DUNLOP

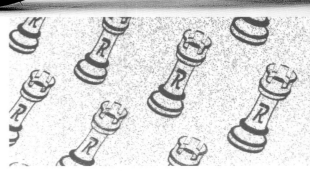

OWNER: Jesse Rooke

YEAR OF BUILD: 2004

ENGINE: Kendall Johnson-built S&S 124-inch Evo-type

FRAME: Jesse Rooke Kali Kruiser

SPECIAL FEATURES: 2004 Chop Shop Tour bike; prototype Drop Starter Slam Clutch Baker Transmission primary; uses first set of Contour Wheels that Roland Sands developed for Performance Machine.

JESSE ROOKE

CHOP SHOP

THE PRINCE OF COOL

ROLAND
SANDS

ROLAND SANDS' *GLORY STOMPER*

You're looking at the first of a new league of custom motorcycles that Roland Sands calls sport choppers. The Glory Stomper went head to head in a *Biker Build-Off* episode against none other than Arlen Ness. No pressure, right Roland?

Starting with a crashed Harley-Davidson Softail, Roland took the neck out of the frame, the Twin Cam motor, and threw the rest away. The Performance Machine Contour wheels, mid-controls, and primary were designed by Roland as part of P.M.'s RSD line. Ohlin's provided the Road and Track front end, Baker took care of the transmission, and Johnny Chop made the bottom of the gas tank while Roland spent time in P.M.'s machining room to create the unique ribbed top of the tank. Believe it or not, the rear Metzeler tire is only a 280, but it sure looks massive hanging out back there.

Special thanks go to Johnny Chop, Tom Foster, Wink Eller, Brett Marshall, the Great Lyndelski, and Perry and Nancy Sands.

ROLAND
SANDS

GLORY STOMPER

OWNER: Roland Sands

YEAR OF BUILD: 2004

ENGINE: Harley-Davidson Twin Cam B, rebuilt by Wink Eller using Edelbrock parts

FRAME: Stock H-D neck, remainder handcrafted by Roland Sands and Brett Marshall

SPECIAL FEATURES: Many billet parts become prototypes for Performance Machine products; oil tank an aluminum casting by noted Utah sculptor Jeff Decker, who also sculpted the "gemon" (good demon) holding the oil line (Roland has a matching tattoo).

ROLAND
SANDS

GLORY STOMPER

His family remembers Roland spinning this small motorized trike around and around in circles like a whirling dervish.
Sands family archive

ROLAND SANDS

THERE IS A LAND THAT LIES SOUTH AND INLAND FROM FABLED SOUTHERN CALIFORNIA BEACHES, A LAND CALLED ORANGE COUNTY. People living within this great expanse of right-wing conservatism, Christian values, and cookie-cutter condos are said to live "behind the Orange curtain." Yet it is behind this very curtain that some of Southern California's wildest custom motorcycles have been born.

In the great industrial wasteland known as LaPalma, there is a massive complex of modern buildings that house Performance Machine. The company was started by Perry Sands and has been leading the way in the design and creation of high quality brakes and wheels for custom bikes for over 35 years.

"I'm infatuated with race bike and car technology both new and vintage, and I think that has more to do with my style of custom bike than anything else."

Starting from a humble shop back in 1970 (the transformed dairy barn featured a large sign that said simply, "Choppers"), Perry, his wife Nancy, and his brother Ted Sands have built an Empire. Their products are constantly honored with design and innovation trophies from the Industry that has spawned them. Their brakes and wheels have more R&D and safety testing behind them than any such products in the world. Today, Performance Machine also provides custom builders with hand and foot controls, mirrors, grips, primary drives, and hundreds of styles of custom wheels and disc brakes. There are over 2,500 parts numbers for wheels alone.

Into this maelstrom of custom creativity was born a son to Perry and Nancy; his name is Roland Sands. Cradled in Long Beach, California, Roland grew up a child of the 1980s, attracted to the X-treme world of dirt bikes, surf punks, and So-Cal's very unique brand of cool. It is this same odd mix of bland religion, morals run amok, Mexi- and Cali-culture that has given the world such engaging media maestros as Jesse James.

Motorcycle oil flows in Roland's veins. His first motorcycle ride was when his dad brought him home from the hospital on his custom Panhead. Perry and Nancy were slim on cars in those days. He remembers riding to Toy Runs sandwiched in between his mom and dad on their faithful FL. Roland graduated

ROLAND
SANDS

Roland was always ready to ride, seen here with his mom and dad, Nancy and Perry Sands.
Sands family archive

to sitting in front of Perry on a dirt bike but accidentally broke his dad's chin on a ride. Ouch! Perry got Roland his own bike after that.

"My first solo ride was in Falbrook," Roland remembers. "I was five years old and my dad's buddy, Punk Wilson, had an XR 100 that he let me ride in the dirt. The next time I rode I broke my arm on a RM 50 that Dad got for me." Figuring the bike was too much for Roland, Perry got him a new bicycle, which he promptly crashed and broke his other arm. Luckily, Roland's parents made their living from designing and fabricating motorcycle parts, so they were more understanding of Roland's passion than most parents might have been. Even Roland's younger sister, Summer, rides her own custom V-Rod. It's a family on two wheels.

Uncle Ted Sands remembers, "Roland was always a livewire, going a mile a minute. Whether he was on a tricycle, bicycle, or motorcycle, he was always testing his vehicles to their maximum limits and was never afraid of getting hurt. I remember he had one of those plastic Big Wheel trikes as a kid, and he could make that thing spin like a dervish! Roland was famous for his Big Wheel slides." Apparently, Roland's mom, Nancy, has kept a running tab of all his broken bones, starting with a broken collarbone when he was being delivered. It's as if he was marked as a hellion right from the start of life. So far, Roland has broken 34 bones, many of which are thanks to the eight years he spent roadracing motorcy-

So far, Roland has broken 34 bones, many of which are thanks to the eight years he spent road racing motorcycles. Note the Performance Machine logo. *Sands family archive*

Young Mr. Sands won the Elf Race Fuels & Lubricants Grand Prix to take the AMA 250 GP championship title, completing the 1998 season with five victories and six additional podium finishes in the 12-race season. *Sands family archive*

OWNER: Roland Sands

YEAR OF BUILD: 2003

ENGINE: Harley-Davidson Twin Cam B with S&S 95-inch kit

FRAME: Stock H-D Softail frame with ugly parts skirted in sheet metal

SPECIAL FEATURES: Wheels anodized blanks that were then cut to shape; like all Roland's bikes, this one's set up to ride.

ROLAND SANDS

EL BORRACHO (THE DRUNK)

Uncle Ted Sands remembers, "Roland was always a live wire going a mile a minute. Whether he was on a tricycle, bicycle, or motorcycle, he was always testing his vehicles to their maximum limits and was never afraid of getting hurt." *Sands family archive*

cles, earning an AMA National 250 Grand Prix Championship title in 1998.

When asked what gave him his driving passion for motorcycles, Roland says, "Motorcycles were all I could remember since I was a kid. I tried to rebel into the skate, snow, surf scene, but there's just nothing cooler and more punk rock than building and riding bikes."

And what bikes he builds. But then Roland is virtually the kid in the custom candy store at Performance Machine. Imagine growing up around all the fantastic CNC machines that can produce any kind of design you could possibly dream up. Interestingly, Roland's first custom creations were race bikes. "I built all my race bikes when I was just getting started. I was like 19 years old then. My first custom Harley was a dirt track, road race–derived Sportster when I was like 22. It went through a bunch of variations and ended up being blue-and-white with 17-inch wheels, upside down front forks, a 1000 kit, and all hard-anodized parts. It was a race bike. It got a *Hotbike* cover in 1998. My first full custom was called *Whiskey Tango*; a TP Engineering–powered, Kosman-framed, rubber-mount Softail in 2002. It was on the cover of *Freeway*, *Hot Rod Bikes,* and a couple of other Euro magazines."

There have been many articles, mostly of the technical variety, in *Easyriders* magazine about Performance Machine's various products. But in the September 2003 issue, we took a close look at PM's in-house custom bike builders, Todd

Roland would often sit in front of Perry on their dirt bike but accidentally broke his dad's chin on a ride. Perry got Roland his own bike after that. *Sands family archive*

Silicato, Peter Vecvannags, and Roland Sands. The article features some of this Triple Threat Talent's (as the article was titled) wild new scoots. When talking about Roland's race-inspired customs, writer Paul Garson was impressed with the designer's racing credits.

"A few years ago Roland won the Elf Race Fuels & Lubricants Grand Prix to take the AMA 250 GP championship title, completing the 1998 season with five victories and six additional podium finishes in the 12-race season." It is clear that Sands knows bikes inside and out.

Roland's style of custom scoot is tough. They are a cross between a road racer and something Mad Max might ride across the Outback. They are also a blend of high tech and old school. Describing the philosophy behind his bikes, Roland sums up his creations as, "Fucking pissed off . . . major attitude without

ROLAND
SANDS

HARD WAY

OWNER: Roland Sands

YEAR OF BUILD: 2003

ENGINE: 124-inch S&S

FRAME: Designed by Roland Sands, built by Jesse Rooke

SPECIAL FEATURES: This was a pivotal bike for Sands. After retiring from racing in 2002 he was depressed. Building this bike snapped him out of it and made him fall in love with bike building.

ROLAND
SANDS

HARD WAY

OWNER: Roland Sands

YEAR OF BUILD: 2005

ENGINE: S&S 124-inch Twin Cam, Jimmy Hannah–built heads, about 135 horsepower

FRAME: Custom-built Chopper Guys

SPECIAL FEATURES: Influenced by Indian Larry; "Borracho's crack-head brother—the most fucked-up combination of stuff I could throw at a bike."

a bunch of gay shit hanging off of them. A bike's platform should be simple, concise, and very rideable. I've always been against bolt-on gadgetry or extreme geometry in the name of shock value. A bike should speak for itself without the paint saying 'Hey, look at me, I want some attention.'"

As a judge of custom bike shows, I can tell you that Roland is right on the mark. The last thing a judge looks at is the paint job. We are more interested in the design and flow of the bike, the attention to detail, the handcrafted, one-off parts. Custom paint is the icing on the cake but not the cake itself. One of the most interesting parts of the design process is without a doubt the process itself. Where do the ideas come from?

ROLAND SANDS

GRANDE MOCO (BIG BOOGER)

"I built all my race bikes when I was just getting started," Roland says. "I was like 19 years old then. My first custom Harley was a dirttrack-roadrace-derived Sportster when I was like 22."

At the drawing board. Roland's style of custom scoot is tough. His bikes are a cross between a road racer and something Mad Max might ride.

When asked to expound upon this Roland is quick to answer, "I'm infatuated with race bike and car technology, both new and vintage, and I think that has more to do with my style of custom bike than anything else. I try not to look to the bike industry for too much influence because I want my designs to be original and not borrow too much from anything that has already been done." This is certainly the case with Roland's designs. I recall a stock Harley Softail that he ingeniously converted into a nasty little Barrio blaster that screamed attitude. It's all about the heart and soul of the ride for Roland.

Case in point, another PM bike to appear in *Easyriders* magazine was Roland's truly sick custom drag machine known as *Hard Way*. The August 2004 issue of *Easyriders* teamed this wicked ride up with one of our sexy models. As the story goes, Roland literally laid pen to wet bar napkin to design the radical frame on *Hard Way*. He handed the drawing to his friend, Jesse Rooke, and two weeks later Jesse delivered the frame right to Roland's house. Everything on this bike was a prototype piece, from the PM Contour primary and midmounted foot pegs, to the GP-style brake calipers. Just for fun, Roland placed the bike's kickstand on the right side instead of the customary left side, just to mess with people's heads.

When asked if any particular bike builder has influenced his process, young Sands told us, "I couldn't help but to be influenced by Indian Larry's style and attitude. His theory of less is more and his sticking to stock geometry confirmed my beliefs that a bike doesn't have to ride like shit to be cool. His personal touches on every motor, and the little details on his bikes were amazing. I aspire to build motors as beautiful as his."

As with all the bike builders in this book, Roland has had a brush with fame through the amazing medium of television. The Discovery Channel featured Roland in an episode of the *Biker Build-Off* series, going up against no less a personage than the King of Customs himself, Mr. Arlen Ness.

It is interesting to note how the marketing minds of television executives work. In the case of the *Biker Build-Off* series, the Discovery Channel top brass realized that they had a hit with motorcycle shows. After all, their *Motorcycle Mania* trilogy and *Monster Garage* (hosted by bike builder Jesse James) were all

The research and design center at Performance Machine in LaPalma, California. Roland is the ultimate kid in the custom candy store.

ROLAND
SANDS

221

ROLAND
SANDS

WHISKEY TANGO

ratings giants. Originally, the Discovery Channel ordered the pilot episode of *Biker Build-Off* and waited to see if the ratings would hold. The series, in case you've somehow missed it, pits two bike builders against each other, each trying to build a custom bike from scratch in 30 days. The first show had Billy Lane of Melbourne, Florida, going up against Roger Bourget of Phoenix, Arizona. Original Productions' Hugh King was once more the producer of the pilot (having produced *Motorcycle Mania* and *Monster Garage*). King decided that it would be interesting to pit young against old, east against west, with low end, old school builder Billy against rich guy, high-end custom maker Bourget. When Billy and Roger rode their *Build-Off* creations to an outdoor bike show in North Carolina for the finale,

OWNER: Roland Sands

YEAR OF BUILD: 2002

ENGINE: Total Performance 121-inch Evo-type

FRAME: Sandy Kosman

SPECIAL FEATURES: First Big Twin custom Roland built; built everything himself; learned to chop on this bike; V-Rod headlight used before first V-Rod hit the streets.

Billy won by popular vote. The mix worked, the ratings were good, and a series was born.

Discovery then ordered another three shows, rather than jumping in with both feet for a full 13 episodes. As mentioned before in this book, Executive Producer Hugh King would often call me for advice on which builders in the country would be good for the show. He wanted a mix of young and old, rich and poor, famous and unknown. Well, the truth of the matter is that there are fewer than 40 custom bike builders in the country who can walk, talk, and build bikes on camera. The problem was that after the first four episodes aired, they were a big success and Discovery wanted 13 more. At two bike builders per episode,

ROLAND
SANDS

WHISKEY TANGO

OWNER: Performance Machines

YEAR OF BUILD: 2004

ENGINE: Total Performance 121-inch Evo-type

FRAME: Highly-modified Chopper Guys

SPECIAL FEATURES: Built to celebrate PM's 35th anniversary; named after building on dairy farm where Roland's father Perry started Performance Machine; "This is not the kind of bike I normally like to build."

that's 26 new builders. Hugh called me in a panic, "We've changed the rules of the show! Now the builders only have 10 days to finish their bikes! Who can I get?"

In short, you get real expert builders, because there are fewer than 30 in this country who can walk, talk, and build a bike on camera in just *10* days! As I helped Hugh with the list for the 13 episodes, I mentioned Roland. After all, he has the might of Performance Machine behind him to help get a 10-day build done. He's young, he's got style, and he's becoming a major name in the custom world.

Roland's episode of the series first aired as this book went to press, but my bet is that the *Build-Off* will only act as a further springboard for the talented 30-year-old. And while many custom builders see participation in the series as a benchmark and sign of "making it" in their profession (and a way to sell T-shirts), Roland will keep his head and continue to fly below the celebrity radar.

He still only builds a few select bikes per year and does it his way. "My approach to bikes is the same as it is with women—quality over quantity any day. Last year I built three bikes, this year I've built two already, and it's only February. Ideally I'd like to hold it down to four or five bikes a year. I'm still holding down a regular job at Performance Machine, so it's tough. I'm getting used to working

ROLAND
SANDS

FLYING PROCESSOR

ROLAND
SANDS

FLYING PROCESSOR

OWNER: Performance Machine

YEAR OF BUILD: 2005

ENGINE: Harley-Davidson V-Rod with Zippers 1320cc Z-Rod kit

FRAME: H-D V-Rod

SPECIAL FEATURES: Prototype for a V-Rod kit Roland is developing for Performance Machine; PM swingarm; gauges frenched into airbox cover; tail section adopted from Kawasaki Supersport road racing bike; one of Roland's personal favorite bikes.

crazy hours all the time, but I don't want to work this hard forever."

Actually, Roland is being very modest. His job at Performance Machine is very important to the company, as he personally designs many of the various parts and products that PM sells. His Contour hand and foot controls have won Excellence in Motorcycling design awards from the V-Twin Expo as has his Contour line of wheels. He is single-handedly changing the look of custom bikes all over the world, whether he'll cop to it or not. When asked about his work with PM, he simply replies, "I've been designing product for Performance Machine for the last 10 years. If you open up the PM catalog, I designed all the wheels, Contour controls, race wheels, Contour brakes, and all that stuff."

Yes, and all that stuff keeps Performance Machine at the top of its game in a very competitive world. The parts Roland designs are always in demand. In fact, there is a three- to six-month wait for his latest designs. His advice to other builders and designers? "Remember, form follows function. It is not the other way around."

So what's it like to be that kid in the candy store? Is Roland living his dreams? "It's a dream I never really considered. I'd given up on my dream of being a Moto GP champion (after 34 broken bones) and I figured I'd just settle

into a nice job at PM, design products, and build some bikes when I had spare time. Next thing I know, people are really digging my stuff, and the bikes are coming out really different and getting a lot of attention.

"I'm really fortunate. I can envision these bikes and have the opportunity to build them. I get to build what I dream and obsess about, so I don't think there's a more real way to live your dream. So, yes, I'm definitely living my dream."

When all is said and done, how will the custom world remember its Prince of Cool? Roland has some thoughts and wishes. "I'd like to be remembered for my design skills, and I'd also really like to expand the (cool) custom market past just the Harley-Davidson V-twin market. How cool would it be to bring back cheap customs like in the 1970s, with in-line fours and make them cool? Let's bring other manufactures into the market and expand it. You know they all want a piece. I'd like to be remembered as the guy with the sharpest pencil, the dude who blended the old with the new and did it right. The guy who brought modern racing technology to the custom market and made it cool. You know, that short guy with the red hair, he looks like a punk kid, but he pulled more trim and built more sick bikes than he knew what to do with, and he could ride the piss out of them. That's the immature perspective. I can't seem to get away from it." ✪

ROLAND
SANDS

PERFORMANCE MACHINE

ROLAND SANDS

PERFORMANCE MACHINE